# JUST FASHION

## Critical Cases on Social Justice in Fashion

*I will give you a talisman. Whenever you are in doubt, or when the self becomes too much with you, apply the following test. Recall the face of the poorest and the weakest man you have ever seen, and ask yourself if the step you contemplate is going to be of any use to him. Will he gain anything by it? Will it restore him to a control over his own life and destiny? In other words, will it lead to swaraj (self-rule) for the hungry and spiritually starving millions? Then you will find your doubts and yourself melting away.*

(Gandhi, "A Note" in Mahatma, VIII, 89, 8-47)

edited by Otto von Busch

ISBN: 978-91-976431-4-6

New York: Selfpassage 2012

## AUTHORS:

Gisela Aguilar
Susana Aguirre
Maureen Brewster
DaMarkis Brown
Cally Carbone
Alessandro Esculapio
Kelsey Allyn Glein
Lauren Gomez
Laura Jane Kenny
Devon Novotnak
Laura Peach
Joanna Petticord
Minna Shim
Otto von Busch

Illustrations by:
Maureen Brewster
Joanna Petticord
Otto von Busch

## BODY MATTERS



## JUST FABRICATION



## POST-SCRIPT

To art theorist Elaine Scarry, beauty and justice are intimately connected through our human perception of symmetry. We are drawn to symmetry intuitively. And we often address injustices in a similar vein; we can feel when something is wrong. Symmetry is a foundation of most traditions of aesthetics, just as balance and proportions. In her book *On Beauty and Being Just*, Scarry accounts for a discussion she had with economist Amartya Sen, where Sen evokes Aristotle's' idea of justice as a perfect cube; equal and proportionate in all directions (Scarry 1999: 64).

However, we can also think of aesthetic expressions that are based on, and even thrive, because of imbalance and disproportions, specifically social ones. Fashion might be one of them. Fashion is fashionable simply because not everyone has access to it cannot be fairly distributed amongst everyone. As Karl Lagerfeld puts it, it is "ephemeral, dangerous and unfair." (Lagerfeld 2007) And it is popular because it is connected to people we admire and look up to – and thus it has nothing to do with the disadvantaged, poor, helpless and ugly. So can there be any connection between fashion and justice? Can fashion somehow address the world's injustices – or can it only feed, and even celebrate, the imbalances of the world? The aim of this book is to start a discussion on these ideas.

What you have before you is a collection of cases that came out of the course "Critical Fashion and Social Justice" at Parsons The New School for Design in New York during fall 2012. The cases act as examples of how fashion, both as a phenomenon and industry, deals with some aspect of social justice, discussing practices, but also putting these practices under a theoretical light. They are not exhaustive examples and the application of theory comes from the probing perspective of fashion. But we see this contribution as the beginning of a discussion and a first effort to place the issues of justice within the discourse and practice of fashion in order to move the discussion beyond the hailed "democratization" of fashion. More people may have access to cheap clothes today, but the mechanisms of inclusion and exclusion are still pervasive. To address these issues through a lens wider than pure consumerism, these texts identify social problems, raise critique and expose systematic contrast in order to examine alternative social arrangements, in a manner similar to what sociologist Gideon Sjoberg has called a "countersystem" approach (Sjoberg et al 2003). The texts act as a point of departure where we have tried to expose some of the ways through which people invested in fashion can address social change and mitigate the injustices we are all part of.

Otto von Busch

# Introduction: Fashion, Justice and Dependence

In everyday life, fashion consumption sometimes seems like a quick and easy fix to almost any social problem. We get a new skin, we feel seen, we feel socially safe and popular and we leave old insecurities behind – we feel we are "on top of the game", among the chosen ones. Yet we all know that this is an ephemeral experience, and at the end of the day it will even further our anxiety. In that way, fashion is an addiction to powerlessness. We acknowledge our reliance on new clothes, preferably made by someone famous, someone in power, someone who shines so bright that some little sparkle will even come onto us down here. Fashion is an atomizing phenomenon in which elitism seems so "natural" to us that we do not even consider its inherent injustices.

Through fashion we think we have equal opportunities, a fair distribution of goods and possibilities, and even that a "democratization" is taking place through fast fashion, as more people have access to a styled life. We are made to believe we have access to fashion while we are simultaneously and bluntly locked out of any decision-making, or any act of empowerment or self-determination, as the goods are already on the hanger awaiting us. We feel we pick the clothes, celebrating our freedom of choice, but we fail to see that someone else has already chosen for us. We are steeped into a system of pacification and almost totalitarian control of what is deemed worthy, valuable and "right". Today, all effects concerning the sensibilities of dress are funneled through the fashion economy, and we come to accept that not everyone is included, as the fashion itself is based on arbitrary exclusion. Exclusion is based not only on monetary assets, but also size, gender, race, body type and abilities.

One of the primal questions on fashion from a social justice perspective concerns agency: how can fashion facilitate social agency, and not undermine it? This means: in what ways can fashion promote autonomy and self-determination, rather than push the consumer into relations of heteronomous dependency? It is thus not a question of leveling the social field

of expression, making everyone dress in uniforms, even though we could say that fashion per se is a sort of uniform. Instead we must examine what relationships of dependency fashion promotes, and consider how the individual can have a say in the ways that these relationships are determined and enacted. Who is included or excluded, who has access and who does not, who has power and who is left powerless? These are questions at the core of social justice.

In philosopher Hannah Arendt's famous study *On Violence,* she expounds on the difference between power and violence and draws distinctions between the two. First, power is the ability to make people act in concert, and secondly, whereas power is an end in itself, violence is only a means to that end (Arendt 1969). Fashion has the power to make us act in concert, but without the feeling that our decisions and tastes are forced upon us. However, that force is acted out in-between us, as a form of social cohesion. Even though the influences or social pressures on us are not violent, it is a stealthy form of violence. In the book *Violence and Social Justice,* political philosopher Vittorio Bufacchi explores how we can be victims of violence, sustain a hurtful transgression of humiliation or a violation of our integrity, even though the act itself may not be violent. Locking someone in a cell and throwing away the key in order to starve the prisoner to death may not be violent itself, but is still an act of violence. As Bufacchi notices: "violence is, by nature, a social act, which ought to be defined within the logic of the appropriate social dynamics", that is, the systematic exploitation and violation of integrity (Bufacchi 2007: 7&29ff)

Even though we may not feel we are excluding anyone, under the cover of fashion we all make judgments of others by their looks, and turn this into a "natural" human phenomenon. But it is easy to overlook that not everyone has the same opportunities. The system is built on the premise that others are excluded, unseen, or uncounted. There is an urgency to reveal this everyday violence, discuss what can be done to stop it, and develop practices that can at least reduce it. A first step can be to discuss critical fashion and social justice at the same time, to mobilize our attention and assets to act in a self-reflective manner and not accept the system of fashion as an external force we cannot change. Sociologists Joe Feagin and Hernán Vera have quoted former secretary general of the United Nations, Dag Hammarskjöld in order to address this: "We are not permitted to choose the frame of our destiny. But what we put in it is ours." They continue:

> "Each member of this society is a part of the systems of oppression, for no one can escape, and all are part of the struggle to maintain or remove these systems. But we can choose which side to be on." (Feagin & Vera 2001: 36)

# MARGINA

# LIZATION

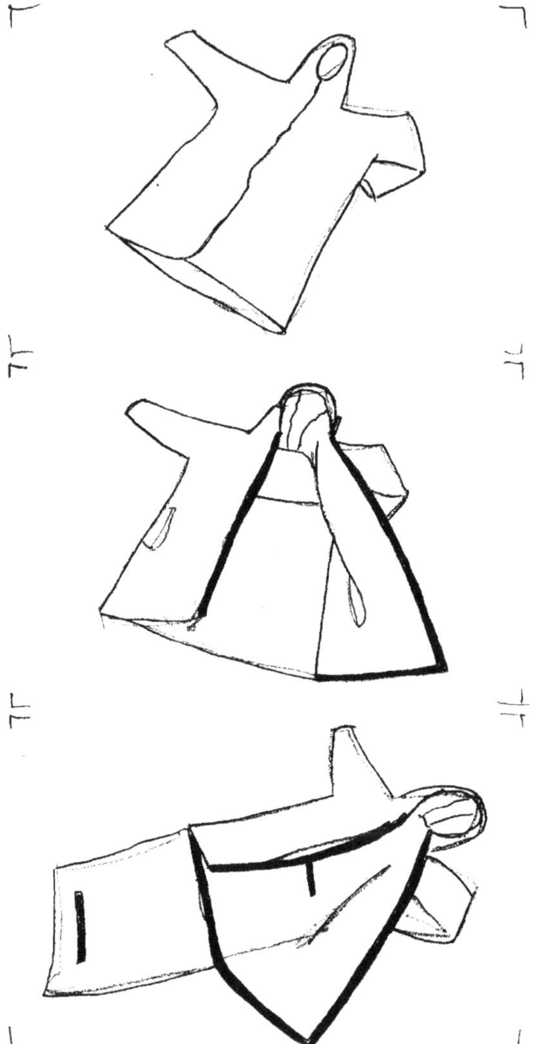

Alessandro Esculapio

# The Empowerment Plan Designs In A Different Voice

The fashion system often promotes unethical practices behind the veneer of glamour, especially when we consider phenomena such as fast fashion, but also realities such as that of luxurious ready-to-wear, traditionally waving the flag of high quality and nonetheless occasionally guilty of exploiting workers [1]. We are often under the impression that ethics has no place in the actual production of garments and this may be in part true, there are, however, important exceptions to the rule.

Rising awareness of the importance of design and visual media in our technology-driven, globalized scenario has also led scholars and practitioners to rethink the role of design in contemporary society. As design scholar Earl Tai points out, if we acknowledge the importance of design nowadays, something that is hardly questionable, especially as we consider the massive presence of fashionable clothing in our everyday life, we must also discuss its role in terms of justice, accessibility and distribution (Tai 2009: 458).

When addressing the broad concept of justice, one inevitably enters the realm of moral philosophy. From Plato and Aristotle onwards, justice has been analyzed from many different viewpoints and almost always theorized through abstract notions of formal rights and rules as well as impartiality and universality. Feminist thinkers, first and foremost Carol Gilligan in her book *In A Different Voice* (1982), questioned this ethical approach and described it as inherently male due to its focus on formal law and responsibility. To complement this approach, she proposed a so-called 'ethic of care', an attitude that in her opinion is typically, though not exclusively, female. While traditional justice is concerned with universal regulatory principles, the ethic of care originates from a view of concrete social relationships as central to the development of one's morality.

## The Empowerment Plan: Design for Social Change

The Empowerment Plan project was started in 2010 by college design student Veronika Scott. As stated in the official website of the project, the Empowerment Plan aims to break the vicious cycle in which most homeless people end up in when they either cannot or do not want to access a shelter and still do not have a place to go at night. In Detroit this is a reality for over 20.000 people, some of which Scott had the chance to meet in person while working in a homeless shelter over a period of five months. She then realized that she wanted to make something about this issue beyond her five-month commitment and thus developed the Empowerment Plan.

The project revolves around the MPWR coat, a self-heated, waterproof coat that transforms into a sleeping bag at night. The coats are made by homeless women, in different sizes and colors according to the personal choice of the 'customers'. A significant contribution came from General Motor's manager of waste reduction effort John Bradburn, who decided to donate 2000 yards of insulating material discarded during the industrial process. While some journalists were sceptical of GM's contribution and suggested that it was a weak attempt at self-promotion, it is undeniable that without their support the project would not have received such wide press coverage. According to Scott's Operations manager Julie Benac, "The new insulation from GM will bring the cost of the coat down by at least 8$". Until now, the coats have in fact been made with generic and nongeneric Thinsulate. In addition to this, different materials were either recycled or donated.

In terms of production the project is almost entirely sustainable. Eight previously homeless women were trained by professional seamstresses to learn to sew and construct the garments. Benac claims that "They have since then learned many valuable skills. They are fully proficient on compound-walking-foot single needle machine, as well as sergers. All the ladies are also cross-trained to perform any operation on the coats, as in a modular manufacturing floor ... The skills they have learned will allow them to go to any manufacturing floor armed with the knowledge and know-how to fit right in". The aim was to create new jobs for those who wanted to be employed and to provide coats for those in need. This is empowering in two ways: both for the women employed, who reacquire self-esteem and financial independence, and for the people living on the streets that do not want or cannot access homeless shelters, who thus not only gain more independence, but also get to interact with the community and other people in their same conditions. This is clearly stated in the manifesto of the project, whose goals are:

- to employ homeless females within the city of Detroit.
- to give coats or the MPWR coat to individuals living on the streets.
- to establish trust and communication with individuals deemed by the shelters as unreachable in the homeless community, for example the mentally impaired.
- to teach sewing manufacturing/ production skills to people that need jobs.
- to offer a sense of pride to the women who have been employed in the production of the coats.

Ordinary people can fund the project through a donation-based system. However, next year the company will launch a for-profit parallel project to keep their non-profit activity running. Among the products they intend to launch, they also wish to commercialize the MPWR coat as sportswear for campers, hikers and so on. Still, the focus will be on the non-profit side of the project: "Not only will we keep our dedication to hiring only homeless women, we intend to promote from within, growing the company from previously homeless women who may then choose to go on for the for-profit. With each coat sold for the for-profit, one coat will be made and donated through the non-profit", Benac states. Veronika Scott and her co-workers are able to cut down the production costs also because they do not have to pay any rent. The studio is in fact located in a shared communal space provided by restaurateur and philanthropist Phillip Cooley, 'Detroit revitalization advocate' [2], who has been actively changing the profile of the city for years by promoting sustainability, good design practices as well as urban projects. Ironically, Cooley is a former model that decided to stop working in the fashion industry out of ethical reasons.

## The Empowerment Plan: A Reading

In an interview for MAKE magazine Veronika Scott stated: "When I started The Empowerment Plan, it was the first time I had to think beyond the scope of just 'user' or 'client'— this had to pertain to a community of individuals. And to me it was no longer just a concept, it was something that I was trying to make happen. So working within the scope of reality was pretty new to me". (MAKE magazine, 07/22/2011)

Scott evaluated the concrete situation and its unique factors through her personal experience at a homeless shelter, something that allowed her to relate to people who lived on the street and to listen to their needs. In a second interview for the website Iamyoungdetroit, she also stated that she continued the project beyond her academic obligations because "people needed, wanted and desired it", thus making clear that her personal feelings and her web of relationships played a major role in her decision.

The key-points of Gilligan's ethic of care are three: it hedges around the ideas of responsibility and relationships rather than formal law; it states that morality has to do with concrete circumstances rather than theoretical abstractions; it states that morality manifests itself not in an abstract set of rules, but rather in everyday moral problems (Larrabee 1993: 242). As philosopher Mary Jeanne Larrabee underlines, "The importance of Gilligan's work is particularly obvious in philosophical moral theory, where the abstractions of ethicists have dominated the field, allowing little if any reference to the reality of people's moral lives". (Larrabee 1993: 5)

As seen above, the main motivation behind Scott's project is indeed doing something about a concrete problem that had not been tackled efficiently by the public bureaucratic system that represents formal justice. This not to say that public institutions or statal law are inefficient per se, but rather to show how we reach social justice more effectively if we complement formal justice with initiatives motivated by feelings of care and empathy. According to feminist theorist Marilyn Friedman, "In its most noble manifestations, care in the public realm would show itself, perhaps, in foreign aid, welfare programs, famine or disaster relief, or other special programs designed to relieve suffering and attend to human needs". (Friedman in Larrabee 1993: 267).

The male and the female perspectives on morality, as Gilligan identifies them, can then work together to bring about concrete changes within a community or a society: "I describe care and justice as two moral perspectives that organize both thinking and feelings and empower the self to take different kinds of action in public as well as private life" (Gilligan in Larrabee 1993: 209) Some scholars, however, have criticized the attitude of Gilligan as too gender-oriented, although she clearly states that the ethic of care is not exclusive of women (Gilligan 1982). On the other hand, Friedman convincingly argues that we need to go beyond the gender division to embrace a "nongendered, nondichotomized, moral framework in which all moral concerns could be expressed". She then states ironically that such a project should be called 'de-moralization of gender'. (Larrabee 1993: 267). At any rate, we must not forget that two goals of the Empowerment Plan explicitly focus on women and that all the people that help Scott to manufacture the coats are women. This partly explains the name of the project, which among other things aspires to provide them with self-esteem and pride. At the same time, those goals sadly remind us that women today still feel the need to be empowered.

What is interesting design-wise is that the MPWR coats preserve the feeling of care with which they are made and transmit it to the wearers, particularly through their sheltering aspect. This also goes back to the relationship between clothes and body, as well as that between fashion and architecture. The MPWR coat is in fact the ultimate house for the body. Scott herself brings up the emotional factor of her design: "The sleeping bag aspect of the coat came out of a more emotional need, strangely enough, rather than a physical one. I added it to address the need of pride. … I added on the sleeping bag of the Element S coat so that those individuals who did not want to be in shelters or whom the shelters could not convince to come inside could have something to keep them alive in the winter, designed in their size in the colors they want and made of new materials that they could claim ownership of". (MAKE magazine, 07/22/2011)

The garment is, so to say, a caring garment, in that it literally takes care of the person who is wearing it (or, concretely speaking, it can save her/his life on a cold night). At the same time, by providing homeless with the choice of color, Scott implicitly recognizes the value of aesthetic discourse in fashion design. While the MPWR coat will hardly become a fashionable garment according to the parameters set by the fashion system [3], it nonetheless allows the wearer to feel "special" and "unique", as well as to participate in the creative process. In this sense the coat is a result of an inclusive and democratic project.

The Empowerment Plan has many points in common with Krzysztof Wodiczko's Interrogative Design Group, a group of designers, artists and activists that "combine art and technology into design while infusing it with emerging cultural issues that play critical roles in our society yet are given the least design attention" [4]. Wodiczko has engaged in the past with projects that specifically tackled the issue of homelessness, most notably the 'Homeless Vehicle Project' featured in the exhibition *This Will Have Been: Art, Love and Politics in the 1980s*. The project, a vehicle that can be pushed around the city, that transforms into a sleeping structure and also includes facilities to wash clothes and store objects, "disturbed conventional views of homelessness...by targeting an occupational subculture of single homeless men (those who survive by redeeming empty cans and bottles for five-cents deposits) as potential user-consumers of an ostentatiously designed object" (Hebdidge 2012). As the MPWR coat is meant to be a design object rather than a provoking art object, it does not bring up issue of consumerism among homeless people, but possibly represents a concrete answer to Wodiczko's provocation.

Projects like the Empowerment Plan show that fashion design is undergoing a redefinition by extending its boundaries far beyond the traditionally elitist, exclusive fashion system. Concepts such as democracy, social awareness and sustainability are reshaping the fashion landscape and bringing in new ideas and approaches. It can then be of help to employ the umbrella-term 'critical fashion' to describe such alternative practices of which the Empowerment Plan is a good example.

Throughout the study case I tried to show how Veronika Scott's project qualifies as critical fashion design and how its social aims can be interpreted through the lens of the feminist ethic of care elaborated by Gilligan and others. I would further argue that a true ethic of care is critical and democratic in itself in that it is inevitably pluralistic and relational. It therefore constitutes a very fruitful framework, or rather a set of ethical attitudes, for the contextualization of critical design that aims at social justice.

Central to the idea of critical design is human value. Boundaries between designers and customers are often blurred in what can be seen as a true collaboration and exchange experience in the name of human relationships. As Gilligan said during a talk at MIT in 2009, "To care is to be present, it's to have a voice, it's to be in a relationship".

I now wish to conclude with the idea of 'design humanism' coined by designer and writer Gui Buonsiepe, which in turn references the concept of humanism expressed by linguist Edward Said. It is essentially what Friedman would consider a 'manifestation of care in the public realm' and also a perfect description of Scott's Empowerment Plan: "Design humanism is the exercise of design activities in order to interpret the needs of social groups, and to develop viable emancipative proposals in the form of material and semiotic artifacts" (Buonsiepe 2009: 213).

**Notes:**

[1]. A case that was given wide press coverage in 2011 was that of Gucci. See for example Alexis Lai's article "Gucci faces 'sweatshop' claims in China", available at http://business.blogs.cnn.com.

[2]. From "HuffPost's Greatest Person of the Day: Phillip Cooley, Detroit Revitalization Advocate", available at http://huffingtonpost.com.

[3]. Ironically, fashion nerds will probably see a resemblance between the MPWR Coat and Maison Martin Margiela's "duvet coat" from their A/W 1999 collection, a slightly different version of which was included in the recent Maison's collection for H&M.

[4]. Manifesto from the Group's website http://interrogative.org/about.

Joanna Petticord

# The Parish Model: Goods Of Conscience

In 2005, Father Andrew O'Connor of Holy Family Church in Castle Hill in the Bronx started a project he called Social Fabric. It was at a retreat in Guatemala that he became aware of the dire poverty level in Guatemala; he was also inspired by the cultural tradition of back-strap weaving among the indigenous communities. "There is 80% malnutrition among the Indian communities of Guatemala, the worst in the Northern Hemisphere, even worse than Haiti," Father O'Connor remarked in an interview, and Social Fabric, he hoped, would help alleviate poverty there (Molloy 2009). Meanwhile in the Bronx, where many have historically struggled economically, Father O'Connor saw a need within his own congregation: the need for jobs. Even before the economic recession of 2008 , the Bronx was one of the poorest urban areas in the United States, and in 2010 "the Bronx remained the poorest urban county in the country"; and Social Fabric became part of a larger project: Goods of Conscience (Roberts 2011). On the Goods of Conscience website, Father O'Connor states: "This initial idea grew into what Goods of Conscience has become today; an apparel line that employs Mayan Indian weavers in Guatemala and underemployed sewers in the Bronx to produce clothing that looks good, feels good and does good." (GOC:2012)

In 2009, Cameron Diaz was featured on the cover of Vogue wearing a pair of shorts from Goods of Conscience. It garnered a mention in the editorial where Anna Wintour called the organization "charitably minded" and the shorts "a personal favorite" (Molloy 2009).

The Goods of Conscience label at the Holy Family Parish provides "through the fair-trade process" 60 to 100 people work, which pays them $8.00 to $14.00 per hour to manufacture the clothing. The handwoven fabric is produced in Guatemala. In boutiques consumers pay $95.00 for a short-sleeved shirt and $775.00 for a coat which one interview says, "reflects the higher cost of human manufacturing" (McCue 2012). The idea of fairness, especially with regard to exchange, appears to be prevalent in the dialogue surrounding Goods of Conscience.

We normally attribute social justice to distributive principles or the fair allocation of rewards and burdens in a society. Social theorist Emile Durkheim was especially concerned with the idea of just exchange. Durkheim believed that the social contract changed according to the development of society which is characterized by its division of labor. Where earlier societies had less division of labor and modern industrial societies more division of labor; the social contract (for many, the key to societal equilibrium) evolved from a blood covenant to the consensual contract, that is, entering into an exchange based on mutual consent (Capeheart & Milovanovic 2007: 31). Importantly, Durkheim observed that "even though two people might freely enter an exchange relation, one may have greater abilities to impose his will on the exchange than the other." (Capeheart & Milovanovic 2007: 31).

Here we can see how Father O'Connor is concerned not only with creating a small-scale system to distribute wealth (rewards) in a structural way by creating work, but also with providing fair compensation through a just contract that practices Durkheim's ideas on social justice. "Justice for Durkheim, should not revolve around consent. Instead it should be connected to social value." (Capeheart & Milovanovic 2007: 31). Goods of Conscience achieves social justice clearly in the production of the clothing, in particular in the sense that "the sum of the efforts necessary to produce the object", part of social value, are adequately exchanged with compensation. As mentioned before, workers at Goods of Conscience earn up to $14.00 per hour. According to the United States Census Bureau, the average per capita income in Bronx County, NY in 2010 was $17, 575 (USCB). At $14.00 per hour it would be possible for workers at Goods of Conscience to make the average per capita income in roughly 250 working days per year. It may be disputed about whether or not this is an average to strive for with the Bronx low economic ranking on the national level.

Although the project conforms to the imaginary structures which potentially created or further aggravated the very conditions that it seeks to address, Father O'Connor's work must be considered in the context of a country which has high unemployment and a county in which 28 percent live under the poverty level. However, to return to a Durkheimian value, it has the potential to create an evolved solidarity that "includes the concerns of other workers within a structure." Solidarity for Durkheim is of primary importance in creating a socially just society (Capeheart & Milovanovic 2007: 30-31). Goods of Conscience not only creates some income for those in need, but more importantly, also plants the seeds for more lasting social change through the bonds of solidarity.

JOBS not JAILS
HOMEBOY

Gisela Aguilar

# "Jobs not Jails": Homeboy Silkscreen Industries

*Community trumps gang, every time.*
Father Greg Boyle

California, once considered the "gang capital of America," has historically been the playground for gang life and violence since the early 20th century. Severe racial tensions arose as an influx of immigrants arrived to the west coast state in the 1920s, which resulted in an enduring legacy of segregation and criminalization of racial minorities. The Zoot Suit riots of the 1930s marked one of the well-documented instances in which racial profiling culminated in a bloody brawl between American servicemen and the "Zoot Suiters." Mexican-American men who developed a fondness for dressing in baggy zoot suits and speaking an English-Spanish slang, were tracked down and beaten by servicemen for their supposed affiliation to gangs. During the 1950s in the Los Angeles region, "small outbreaks of violence erupted in schoolyards and in neighborhood parks [...] based on competing school or neighborhood loyalties, ethnic and racial identities, as well as on the structured activities of incorporated gangs looking to increase territory or reputation" (Ides 2009: 287). The media subsequently labeled these minor incidents as gang activity.

Throughout the following decades, formal gangs such as Calle 18 (1960s), Bloods (1970s), Crips (1970s), and MS-13 (1980s) began to emerge and stake their territory throughout Southern California (Gangs or Us 2012). The products of social, racial, and political inequality, individuals sought out to become gang members because of the social entitlements that were negated to them. Gang culture revolved around the "Three R's", Reputation, Respect, and Retaliation/Revenge (Gangs or Us 2012).

This case study takes a closer look at the ongoing "war on youth" prevalent in the United States, through an analysis of the gang intervention organization Homeboy Industries. Specifically, I ask: how does this organization aim at unveiling the deeper social issues that have enabled gang culture in Los Angeles to endure for more than half a century? What social entitlements are these gang members denied by society? Homeboy Industries attempts to rectify this injustice through an emphasis on education, community, and employment in order to create an environment that fosters productivity, a sense of self-worth and accomplishment for at-risk youths (Giroux 2012). The exemplary efforts of Homeboy Industries, one of Los Angeles' most renowned gang intervention and re-entry centers revolves around its mantras, "Jobs not Jails," and "Nothing stops a bullet like a job" to succinctly work toward giving socially marginalized and neglected youth a chance.

In 1988, Father Greg Boyle who was part of a Catholic parish in the rough Los Angeles neighborhood of Boyle Heights, created "Jobs For a Future" (JFF), a simple job program started as a way to provide an alternative to gang life (Homeboy Industries 2012). The success of the program took JFF out of the parish confines and evolved into what is now known as Homeboy Industries, an independent nonprofit organization located in downtown Los Angeles. Homeboy's "Jobs not Jails" mantra is rooted in Father Boyle's commitment to social justice by providing a "therapeutic community where those ready to move beyond gangs voluntarily" make the decision to empower themselves through the various job opportunities presented to them. Homeboy Industries has four small business branches: Homeboy Bakery, Homegirl Café & Catering, Homeboy/Homegirl Merchandise, and lastly the focus of my case study, Homeboy Silkscreen & Embroidery. Each small business enterprise is composed of a work force of ex-gang members, convicts, and at-risk youth who, through job placement and training sessions, utilize concrete skills to earn wages and cultivate their resume and professional work experiences.

Homeboy Silkscreen & Embroidery, the bread and butter of Homeboy Industries, was established in 1996 as a silkscreen enterprise which prints custom logos on clothing and also provides embroidery services for commercial and non-commercial clientele (Homeboy Silkscreen & Embroidery 2012). With annual sales and revenue of over $1 million, Homeboy Silkscreen employs over 500 ex-convicts and rival gang members who learn "the fundamentals while developing a work ethic working side by side with their enemies" (California Green Solutions 2012). For Homeboy Silkscreen, the commercial success of the business is a direct result of the value placed not only on the end product but also on each individual that makes up that business. Social justice and commerce, in this instance, adopt a symbiotic relationship where clients and well as the Homeboy employees prosper. The genesis of Homeboy Industries was prompted by Father Boyle's immersion in a community plagued by social injustices. It was through this intimate observation of the day-to-day experiences and hardships for his community that led him to search for a way to fill in the gap for what was missing – opportunities. These new possibilities manifested themselves through job training and employment opportunities which not only yielded a sense of responsibility, accomplishment, and confidence but also resulted in an alternative to gang life by building social ties and connections outside of the gang environment. As political theorist John Alexander elaborates when discussing economist Amartya Sen's capabilities approach to justice, "social justice consists in creating the greatest possible condition for the realization of basic capabilities for all" (Alexander 2008: 1). Viewed through the lens offered by the capabilities approach, Homeboy Industries strives to provide an environment in which members can explore and build their own capabilities and offer opportunities that were not otherwise available to them. Similarly, through the lens of liberation sociology, Homeboy Industries embodies the goals of empowering subjugated and oppressed people through knowledge as a way to better their positions in life (Feagin & Vera 2001: 10).

Indeed, Homeboy Silkscreen provides a safe and educational environment that fosters confidence, work ethic, and self-actualization, but as the cultural critic Henry Giroux argues, it is crucial that we focus not only on what these kinds of organizations are doing but also what is the larger social "wrong" that they address? (Giroux 2012). Why do, in this instance, minority youths turn to violence and gang life? How does our social tendency to ignore and expect nothing from this group enable this kind of criminal activity to continue? It is the larger socio-political, economic, and racial histories of this country that ultimately proliferate the ostracism of these communities. Just as Giroux asked what kind of society produces individuals who kill innocent youths, in this case we must ask who has access to education, employment, and the opportunity for self-actualization? Who is denied these necessities and why? Father Boyle's organization is rooted in remedying these injustices through the establishment of a community which embraces and encourages troubled youth by providing them with the tools and knowledge they have normally been negated. Homeboy Industries thus addresses this "war on youth" by recognizing that self-actualization alleviates part of the "ongoing conditions of uncertainty regarding their [youths] education, health care, employment and also their future" (Giroux 2012). If we look at the ex-convicts and ex-gang members that willingly join Homeboy Industries, what does this tell us? When given the opportunity, they want to - and will - take it.

Cally Carbone

# Laundry Love Project: Clean Clothes Create Opportunities

*If I had clean clothes I think people would treat me as a human being*
T-Bone, the individual credited as the founding spark for the project

According to a study reported by USA Today in 2009, "1.6 million unduplicated persons used transitional housing or emergency shelters" (National Coalition for the Homeless 2009). There are basic necessities and opportunities that are lacking because of living in transitional or emergency housing. Many charities and foundations have set out to help those who are homeless in many ways, even with addressing a practice many take for granted, laundry.

The story of the Laundry Love Project begins with a socially active group in Ventura, California and their relationship with one homeless man known as T-Bone. While trying to reach out to the local homeless community, the group propelled their initiative through their rapport with T-Bone. When asked how they could come alongside his life, his answer, shared above, was a simple, impactful phrase and is attributed to the launch of the open-source project and its purpose still today.

> Every single Laundry Love effort…is attached to this man, his words, his story, his life, are not uncommon to many others. Our creative and collective energy in sustaining and expanding this idea to you and many others like you remind us that every human being has tremendous worth, and when we share life with another human being that life could spark an idea that ends up caring for thousands. T-Bone was that founding spark (Laundry Love 2003).

The founding group, JustOne, the creator and administrator of Laundry Love, now located in Portland, Oregon, established the project as open-source, so people and groups all over the country and world, for that matter, can establish outreach to their local communities under the Laundry Love name. The mission of the project is to aid community members living in poverty with laundry help and more.

> Laundry Love is an initiative of JustOne in partnership with diverse individuals and groups throughout the U.S. In collaboration with local laundromats the Laundry Love initiative helps to wash the clothes and bedding of the individual and/or family living in poverty. The typical guest/friend to Laundry Love is either homeless, living in vehicles, dwelling in weekly/monthly rated motels or low-income apartments and/or transitional shelters, undocumented workers and immigrant families. The Laundry Love initiative goes beyond clean clothing; Laundry Love seeks to nurture the health, hygiene, economic, and relational well being of each person (Ibid).

Currently there are 130 locations in the United States where Laundry Love projects have been established, and as of 2012, the outreach has extended internationally to Chennai, India, where four Laundry Love projects operate (Eye See 2012). Furthermore, looking at the project's social media platforms, there are frequently people commenting or asking directly about how to establish an Laundry Love in their local area. It is clearly a rapidly expanding project.

Approaching the Laundry Love Project through the principles of capabilities and opportunities as outlined by Amartya Sen will highlight social justice nature of the initiative. "Sen's idea that development is not merely economic growth, but is also an expansion of people's capabilities to be and to do certain valuable things is the starting point of the Human Development paradigm" (Alexander 2008: 59). To begin to analyze with this idea, it is best to describe what Sen considers as capabilities. Simultaneously, it is necessary to digress one level back into Sen's concepts to first understand his outline of the relationship of functionings and capabilities. Sen considers "not only basic functionings like nutrients, life expectancy, health, and education, but also complex functionings like self-respect, social recognition and political participation which are relevant to the assessment of well-being" (Ibid: 57). From functionings the establishment of capabilities comes, Sen expresses that capabilities are the combination of "functionings that a person can achieve or could have achieved...Capabilities therefore stand for the extent of freedom that a person has in order to achieve different functionings" (Ibid: 57). Capabilities can also be comprehended as opportunities. To relate these notions to the Laundry Love Project is to take into consideration not what the volunteers for the initiative provide, but the people who are helped by Laundry Love. One could say that clean clothing is a matter of health, but it is imperative to also examine what Sen detailed as complex necessities for human well being, mainly self-respect and social recognition.

> According to president and founder of the JustOne organization, Greg Russinger, a significant burden is placed on the post-elementary school aged children without access to clean clothes. Teasing and bullying in schools can lead to dropouts and failed educational opportunities. Laundry Love helps alleviate the emotional weight on the children going to school by helping them have access to clean clothes (Eye See 2012).

Russinger's example of school-aged children is striking, but should not discount the feelings of adults. Contemplating T-Bone's poignant answer to the founding members question, illustrates the social need and desire for anyone to have clean clothing. Simply, the initiative helps to bring dignity and opportunity for those in the respective Laundry Love communities and living in poverty. Laundry Love has expanded the capability for people to freely (as in freedom, not cost) wash their clothing. Through Sen's model, they are able to achieve clean clothing because of the capabilities provided by Laundry Love. From Alexander's interpretation of Sen's theory of justice, "freedoms and opportunities generated by public goods are results of effective freedom brought about by interventions of responsible communities and governments" (Alexander 2008: 59).

The various Laundry Love Projects of course adhere to the founding ideologies established by JustOne, especially in details as to how and where the Laundry Love logo is used; but each localized project, by design, is able to assist communities uniquely and most provide human care opportunities beyond the obvious clean laundry, though that is always the main focus. To demonstrate these points, two projects easily highlight the ideals of the project and local concerns, Laundry Love Santa Ana in Santa Ana, California and Laundry Love Project by Current of Tampa Bay, Inc. in Tampa Bay Florida.

> **Laundry Love Santa Ana,** http://www.laundrylovesantaana.com
> Santa Ana, California
> Established in 2009 – 1 Laundromat
> "We are a coalition of non profits, churches, social entrepreneurs, businesspeople, artists and dreamers joined together by a desire to listen to the needs of Santa Ana and respond accordingly".

> **Laundry Love Project by Current of Tampa Bay,** http://www.laundrybycurrent.org
> Florida, Ohio and Nevada
> Established in 2009 – 13 FL Laundromats, 8 OH Laundromats, 1 NV Laundromat
> "For those living below the poverty line, washing clothes regularly presents both a logistical problem and a financial hardship. We partner with local laundromats, which become a place of relief for those living in shelters, motels, cars and on the streets when volunteers arrive to help wash clothes, pay for laundry fees, visit with the participants and entertain their children".

Santa Ana volunteer Scott Overpeck when interviewed by a local Santa Ana website described how

> he believes there's a deeply attractive appeal to a project like Laundry Love that's different from other charity initiatives like working in a soup kitchen, in part, because laundry is a long and tedious process. 'So there's a lot of time to sit there and invest in people's lives. It forces interaction,' he said. 'Barriers are broken down. I saw an accountant who came out to volunteer and he saw

> another accountant standing in line to get his laundry done. Six months ago, they could have been competitors or co-workers. You stop viewing the people we're serving as 'others," Overpeck added. 'Rather, they're just people in different situations right now. [Laundry Love events are] like going to hang out with friends, rather than serving a population' (Ha and Kim, 2011).

Much of the success of Current's Laundry Love project is attributed to the group's founder, which can be read in a local Tampa Bay Times article:

> For some people, clean laundry is a luxury, said Current founder Jason Sowell, 31. He says the group's goal is to show people they are loved by helping them meet a tangible need...'He's changing people's lives,' said Brian Butler, a volunteer [who also] said he wanted to do something that helped restore dignity to those in need (Parker 2010).

No matter where the Laundry Love Project is located and no matter what individual or group is overseeing the local effort, the ideals of the projects remain constant. Their goal is to seek social justice through establishing opportunities for what most consider a basic human task/need and make the act of clean laundry available to those for whom the process may be a financial burden. The atmosphere that is created within the laundromat during each project's time spent helping clean what needs to be washed, is one of love and recognition for each person's well-being. For it is through respect and dignity that we can realize everyone is a human being.

Laura Jane Kenny

# Dress for Success Makes a Stand for Right Suits

Dress is important. This idea is generally accepted in our society and can be supported with the endless advice given to those trying to figure out what to wear while making a first impression. Women often stress about the length of their skirt on the first date fearing that it will reveal the "wrong" idea about their morals. When we look at the dress guidelines for interviews, the stress climbs even higher. While the importance of dress in the role of the first impression is noted in these circumstances, the impact goes even deeper as we see in Diane M. Turner-Bowker's article, "How Can You Pull Yourself Up by Your Bootstraps, if you Don't have Boots? Work-Appropriate Clothing for Poor Women." In this article, Turner-Bowker notes that clothing plays an important role not only by significantly increasing the chances in getting hired, but it also affects other aspects of a poor woman's life, such as their ability to win a court trial (Turner-Bowker 2001). This would suggest that clothing is something quite serious. Dress for Success, an international not-for-profit organization that aids disadvantaged women by providing them with professional attire, serves as an interesting case for our understanding of the importance of design and appearance while also letting us explore the impacts of these pressures.

Design scholar Earl Tai argues in his article "A Case for Distributive Justice in Design" that design and visual concerns should not be cast into the category of luxuries or the nonessential (Tai 2009). Dress for Success surely supports the idea that visual culture should not be limited to the realms of luxury. Tai suggests that in a time and era where visual culture is one of the main forms of communication, that "we would be hard pressed to argue that the medium only operates at the level of luxury, for the very foundations of knowledge are shaped by the medium" (Tai 2009: 457). Tai explains that design and the importance of visual culture is such an essential part of how we interpret information, that its importance must be recognized also from a perspective of justice. The creation of a company like Dress for Success suggests that professional attire is necessity if one is attempting to secure a job of a certain caliber. Diane M. Turner-Bowker also notes the importance of dressing and visual culture as she notes that,

> Clothing plays a role in impression formation and may affect poor women's ability to obtain a good job. Style of dress affects perceptions of, expectations for, and responses to job applicants. Clothing worn by a job applicant is a sign of status, power, and ability and may determine success on the interview and/or on the job. Most poor women lack the financial resources necessary to enhance their outward appearance as an impression management technique (Turner-Bowker 2001).

Turner-Bowker further notes that some studies have shown that clothing can have a greater influence on someone's ability to become hired than one's personal physical appearance, influencing the interviewee on factors such as credibility, attractiveness, compliance and power. These studies would suggest that clothing, especially when it is worn in efforts to secure a job, is incredibly important.

Dress for Success, created in 1997 in New York City, provides each client with one suit when they have a job interview and supplies a second suit or separates when the client finds work. The organization also provides women with other support for the transition into a new work position, such as counseling, in order to help women maintain their jobs. Dress for Success was initiated by Nancy Lublin, a graduate of Brown University and Oxford University. Lublin started the organization while attending law school full time in 1995. When left with an $5,000 inheritance from her great-grandfather Poppy Max, she decided to use his money to honor his memory by creating an organization that could offer aid to those trying to begin new careers. Lublin is also the creator of the non-for-profit DoSomething.org which encourages and aids young people who are seeking to make a positive difference in their communities. Dress for Success has grown immensely has now been launched in more than 100 cities in eight countries.

While Dress for Success is providing a small solution to the inequalities in modern society, the solution it seeks to solve should be addressed. Is it just that clothing, and a certain type of clothing that requires a great deal of monetary resources in order to own, is more or less socially required in order for a person to socially progress in their career? It seems that our modern culture requires certain economic means and resources from individuals as a starting point. Your dress needs to offer a certain professionalism that requires the ability to afford such garments before your ability as a worker is considered. It is also interesting to note that this clothing that is required might not even be the clothing that will be worn during this work. A person interviewing for a job where business casual clothing is acceptable often still needs to wear a suit to an interview. This demands an interview suit--a seemingly useless garment that is only worn to prove one's professional capabilities. Even though this sort of suit is required in order to interview in, it is not provided for those from a disadvantage background from any governmental source, creating a gap between communities who own suits and those who don't. The existence of Dress for Success shows how clothing can be one representation not only of economic disparity but of an economic wall that is hard to jump. One cannot make the money to buy such a suit unless they have the job but they cannot get the job unless they have the suit. And while the efforts and solution that Dress for Success provides is notable and really quite incredible, it is saddening to know that our economy leaves so many without the tools to bridge such a gap.

The creation of a non-for-profit like Dress for Success can be seen as a socially just cause. The powers at play and factors that are present in society that create such disparity in dress are most likely not just. How then do we deal with the inequalities at hand? As a lens for observing social justice, sociologists Loretta Capeheart and Dragan Milovanovic encourages us to examine justice as it affects the whole of society and not only the individual. While ways of achieving these goals can be debated and have been debated for centuries, we should take a pinch of this logic when looking at the problem at hand: certain clothing is required in order to obtain professional success yet these clothes are not available to all. Capeheart and Milovanovic suggest that, "Social justice must include an understanding of the interactions within and between a multitude of people..it requires the consideration of and sensitivity to all voices and all concerns (Capehart 2007)."How then do we listen to all voices when it comes to the pressure of having the right professional clothing? Perhaps this needs to be an exploration into the reasons why suits are required for interviews. Maybe a solution for all includes a cross-socioeconomic class dialogue about the influence of dress. Or perhaps this just requires further funding from the state to help the disadvantage to afford suits to wear to interviews. Yet, maybe it is the conversation itself that needs to be encouraged.

The search for a solution when it comes to socially just clothing highlights the inequalities around us, down to our very threads. It is these spotlights that will help us to continue to look at disparities with a hope for a creative solution that requires the discussion and insight from all of those involved and perhaps even from those who are left out.

Joanna Petticord

# Homeward Bound: Studio Orta

Between the late 80's and early 1990's hundreds of thousands of Kurds fled violent turmoil in Northern Iraq and surrounding areas, flooding into Turkey and on to Western Europe (Greenhouse 1989). It was in 1990 that Lucy Orta began working on "Refuge Wear"; a series of parka-like garments which transform into tents. The project was initiated in order to draw attention to the plight of refugees seeking asylum in Western Democracies who had seemingly "forgotten about the Kurd's plight" (Greenhouse 1989). In analyzing the case of Studio Orta, made up of Lucy Orta, Jorge Orta and other collaborators, through the lens of social justice, it may at first appear as though the injustice that the Ortas tried to address in this project was the condition of the refugee population in Western Europe. In this instance, however, the wrong addressed by Refuge Wear was not just the situation of refugees, but significantly the absence of discussion or recognition of their condition.

To "represent what is not being discussed" is one of a few approaches used by Studio Orta, the joint project run by Lucy and Jorge Orta. Their work, which is part fashion, part activism, part instillation art, part design and part community organizing, but usually polemic and at some point either in ideation or production or in viewing, participatory. This makes their work a defier of classification (Graham 2007: 115). In the couples' dynamic catalogue of work, a range of contemporary global social issues from organ donation to water rights are addressed. The result of their collaborations, workshops and thinking on these issues are manifested physically and presented as statements, calls to action and/or playful design solutions (which are often wearable).

Studio Orta, the husband-wife duo, formed in 1991. Both had some history of social activism and an inclination to, or in Jorge's case, were already experimenting with ways of engaging in social justice activism through art (Graham 2007: 112). His personal ethic of social justice was rooted in "youth movement ideologies, in particular the obsession that we needed to build a more equitable world", as well as Liberation Theology (Graham 2007: 112).

Jorge grew up and spent the early part of his professional life in Rosario, Argentina. Limited by the period of conservative dictatorship between 1976 and 1983, Jorge worked to create new systems for the dissemination of art and ideas, an endeavor that the Ortas still pursue and even regard as a central goal (Graham 2007: 113).

One way to examine Studio Orta's work can be through a lens of social justice, and examine whether Studio Orta can be seen as an autonomous entity based on Greek philosopher Cornelius Castoriadis's work on the intersection between philosophy, politics and autonomy (Castoriadis 1992). I would like to consider potential criticisms, and finally, because the example of Studio Orta is unique in that the concepts or issues that they focus on explicitly related to the form of the final product; I will attempt to asses some of Orta's projects through the lens of artist and designer Krzysztof Wodiczko's concept of "interrogative design" (Wodiczko 1999).

The desire to create a more equitable world can be cited as a reason for the Orta's "socially motivated process and outcomes". A socially committed idea of equality usually implies a contractual relation to the idea of social justice, and this was one of the central principles of legal philosopher John Rawls conception of justice. For Rawls, the social contract was not an entity arrived at in order to counter the base nature of human society, violent or not, but rather an "original position". In other words, in order to avoid bias, the terms of the contract would be arrived at an ignorance of positions of advantage, and in this way an equitable society could thrive (Capeheart & Milovanovic 2007: 19). It may be particularly interesting that two of Rawls' stipulations for equality were freedom of speech and assembly; which were severely limited during Jorge Orta's early time in Argentina, due to the junta.

It is clear from that Studio Orta is committed to imagining a more equitable world and to, at least conceptually, dismantle instituted inequalities. In order to consider change on this scale it may be helpful to utilize some of the ideas of Cornelius Castoriadis; specifically his ideas about autonomy and the imaginary in relation to social change. Castoriadis approaches social change from the notion that the psyche of the individual and the social are continually recreating each other. It is only when the "radical imagination of the psyche seeps through the successive layers of the social armor which cover it...and which constitute the individual that the singular human being can have, in return, an independent action in society." (Castoriadis 1992: 146). In order to do this, Castoriadis would say, the individual must be autonomous, must have "free[d] the radical imagination" through "the formation of a reflective and deliberate instance of true subjectivity" (Castoriadis 1992: 164). In other words, the individual must devise for him or herself, through the act of self-reflection, an own set of laws derived from true subjective deliberation, apart from any external and transcendental "other" (heteronomy). It is in this way that the individual or collective can question the social imaginary and "with the same stroke" create "a new type of society and a new type of individual" (Castoriadis 1992: 166).

I would argue that this is one of the several levels on which Studio Orta aims to work. The Ortas, using interrogative participatory processes, aims to engage the overall institutional processes of society in order to highlight and address social injustices. Through workshops, collective creation and collaboration, Studio Orta not only transgresses the traditional imaginary of the art world or the fashion industry by removing the artist/designer form the pedestal, but also by engaging in politics, which is in itself "a project of autonomy" (Castoriadis 1992: 169). One approach that the Orta's delineate as a primary method of making their work is that they operate not as individuals but as "facilitators of a process for communicating the sentiment, or feeling or the direction of the group" (Graham 2007:115). Jorg explains that "the issue of investigation in this practice is the communal sentiment" (Graham 2007: 115). It is this sort of reflective deliberation and collective participation that Castoriadis might say frees the radical imaginary. From this perspective, Studio Orta's process alone is a vital aspect in precipitating social change.

That is not to say that there are potential drawbacks or criticisms to Jorge and Lucy Orta's art. The work of Studio Orta may be seen in private galleries and museums which could be considered exclusive. It might be simple to reason, viewing the work as an object in the context of the gallery that the social whole is not being addressed due to limited accessibility. As noted by scholars Loretta Capeheart and Dragan Milovanovic, "social justice is concerned not in the narrow focus of what is just for the individual alone, but what is just for the social whole." (Capeheart & Milovanovic 2007: 2). Admittedly one issue in the exposition of the artworks has been the lack of gallery and curatorial interest, until recently, in the collective and collaborative process behind the material object (Graham 2007); which, one could argue is the part of their work which provides the most potency in terms of social justice and social change.

While some awkwardness appears to persist in the relationship of "in-situ" artwork and the instituted modes of presentation, Lucy Orta insists that the "object is really important and can speak for itself. It is an extension of the collaborative process, enabling us to communicate to a wider public these very huge issues." (Graham 2007: 113) She cites 'Refuge Wear - Habitent' as a prime example: "This portable shelter was created back in the early 1990's, it has subsequently travelled around the world and is the most published and exhibited artwork from our archive. It was made at a time when homelessness was not part of public discourse, but should have been, now fifteen years later we see tent cities cropping up all over france surrounded by unprecedented media attention" (Graham 2007: 113).

Krzysztof Wodiczko's concept of "interrogative design" largely resonates with the ideas of Studio Orta, where the object in addition to the process stands up to the challenge of the social justice analysis. Orta's Refuge Wear project remains an excellent example. Wodiczko stipulates that interrogative design "takes a risk, explores, articulates and responds to the questionable conditions of life in today's world" (Wodiczko 1999: 16),and that is precisely embodied in the process and product of Studio Orta. The Refuge Wear project, took a risk by transgressing the bounds of art or fashion at the time and articulated an injustice in the world: in this case it was the conditions of refugees fleeing to western Europe without homes, and homelessness in general. The interrogative design, Wodiczko says, must "'attract while scandalizing and demand hope that its function will become obsolete." (Wodiczko 1999: 16). As mentioned- Refuge Wear is the most published and exhibited work in the Orta's archive. In addition to its publicized history because of its apparent interdisciplinary nature (somewhere in between art, design, and fashion) it must have caught the eye of a broader scope of viewers - what the Ortas call the work's "contamination" (Graham 2007: 115). The project was formally attractive and publicized and yet it criticized "the conditions of which it [was] born", the vulnerable state of the refugees and the homeless, and the impetus for its creation. As an object and as a piece of interrogative design, the Refuge Wear project is a successful piece of design from start to finish.

While it did not actually provide and didn't even mean to provide housing for every refugee, it addresses the "wrong" that it targeted, which was the lack of discussion towards more just conditions for refugees and the homeless. It is through the participatory and reflective processes at work that Studio Orta enacts social change dynamically. Although the impacts of the work of Studio Orta may not be overly perceptible, Studio Orta has equipped us with some conceptual tools which may help us recreate society in a more self-reflective manner, in order to alter the conditions of injustice.

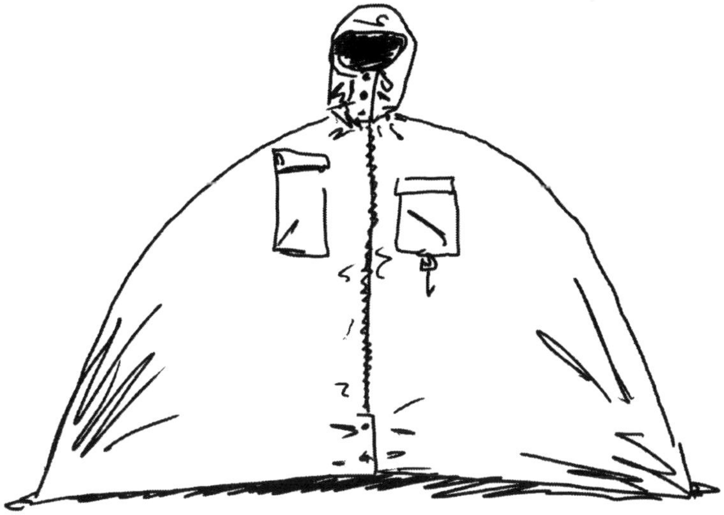

ERNO PRAGMATICO
FONDO. LOS

Susana Aguirre

# Addressing Forced Sterilization: Articulo 6

Peruvian designer Lucia Cuba graduated from the MFA Fashion Design and Society program at Parsons the New School for Design in 2012 with the thesis collection, Articulo 6: Narratives of Gender Strength and Politics. Fusing her talent as a designer with an investment in creating new channels of social and cultural discourse, Cuba sees fashion as a platform for activism and thoughtful design. With Articulo 6, Cuba aims to raise awareness and action around women's rights and social justice. Specifically, the project generates dialogue around the forced sterilization of thousands of women between 1996 and 2000 in Peru.

Articulo 6 is the sixth article within the second chapter of the General Health Law of Peru enacted in 1997 by the then president Alberto Fujimori. It states, "all persons have the right to choose freely the contraceptive methods they prefer, and to receive appropriate information on the methods available and the risks" (Articulo6).

More than 300,000 women and 16,000 men were sterilized under a birth control policy applied by Fujimori. Named the 'Reproductive health and family planification program," it encompassed a nationwide campaign which sought to educate families on reproductive issues and provide health services. In reality, the campaign's methods of birth control targeted the women and men of impoverished and marginalized urban areas and rural communities in the Andean and Amazon regions of the country. The state-run public health program conducted surgical contraceptive procedures without consent, under forced pressure and unsanitary conditions.

In 2001, after the fall of Fujimori in 2000 in light of pervasive corruption and human rights violations during his presidency, and within the context of the creation of the Truth and Reconciliation Commission of Peru (which sought to document and bring to justice the human rights violations that occurred during the internal conflict that consumed the country from the 1980s to late 1990s), 12 women brought the ignored case to the public eye by denouncing the actions taken by the state which violated their rights.

As part of the project, Cuba created a website, Articulo6.pe, in which the designer streams news, images, and videos about the case and her designs. One such video, "We have woken up," is a powerful visual testimony from Aurelia Paccohuanca and Micaela Flores, two women from the town of Anta, Cusco, who have spoken about their experience. During the video, one of the two women mentions how the doctors: "grabbed me by the arms," after she had explicitly told them she did not want the procedure. Waking up from the anesthesia, once the procedure was done, her memory is of women screaming and crying all around her laying on the floor—"They'd put them on the ground, not even on a bed!"

Cuba's Articulo 6 is a collection of 34 pieces that, through form and cloth, articulate the narratives of Peruvians affected by this case. The garments are made out of cotton twill and cotton canvas, making use of prints and embroidery to articulate the "uniformization and militarization of a public policy," the project's website states. Inspired by the pollera, or skirt, used by many women of Andean decent, the construction and silhouettes of the garments aim to represent "the strength and capacity of victims to defend themselves and overcome the irreversible while the images and symbols printed in the fabrics comment on the universe of institutions, activists, press and characters related to the case" (Articulo6).

The looks are unique iterations of pollera skirts, structured blouses, cropped coats and sashes that repeatedly wrap around the body. One such look in an opaque mustard color consists of a deconstructed pollera with long pleats in the front while the back exposes various shorter layers of the skirt through the effect of being ripped apart. One look in burgundy includes a sash embroidered with phrases concerning the case, wrapping around the body numerous times and trapping the arms in its hold. In yet another look, the pleats of a blue pollera are sewed together at the bottom of the skirt, evoking tubal ligation. Other pieces use print to expose imagery of the scarred female body, a photograph of ex-president Fujimori as a boy in uniform, and the text of Articulo 6 both in Spanish and in Quechua, the native language of Andean women.

Polish artist Krzysztof Wodiczko proposes that the concept of interrogative design is that which "takes risk, explores, articulates, and responds to the questionable conditions of life in today's world, and does so in a questioning manner" (Wodiczko 1999: 16). With Articulo 6, Cuba explores the lived experiences of women and their families affected by the state run campaign, articulates in cloth the violation of their rights and questions the state and society's failure to effectively address the case.

In doing so, and by creating actions aimed to interact with the public including performances, film and workshops, Cuba aims to "bring this case to the forefront of public opinion and raise awareness of the need to respect, remember and bring justice to those affected by this vertical and discriminatory public policy that must not be repeated" (Articulo 6). Her design ethos, then, speaks to Wodiczko's belief that interrogative design should serve as "motivation for critical judgment towards the present and past to secure a vision for a better future," (Wodiczko 1999: 16).

Interrogative design isn't a solution, but a vehicle by which society can learn, approach,and act upon issues of injustice in a sensitive and thoughtful manner. Design, which in Cuba's case includes dress design and art installations, has the power to allow people to experience in a particularly impactful way "the experience of pain and the hope of recovery" (Wodiczko 1999: 16). Cuba's approach to fashion design wishes to foster awareness, instigate action and create spaces for dialogue and inclusion.

The forced sterilization of women under president Fujimori in the 1990s has been brought to the national spotlight through activism and within the political arena. What occurred to thousands of Peruvian women has been documented through different mediums: as text and audio-visual testimonies within the Truth Commission in Peru or in the work by French photographer Pierre-Yves Ginet (see. The Dissident Women of Anta in PierreYvesGinet-photos.com). Human rights advocates have worked throughout the years to bring justice and a voice to the forgotten women and men involved in this case. Cuba's project continues this work and paves new paths for the articulation of this and other social issues. The case's report has been taken to the public prosecutor's office twice, having been dismissed both times. In March 2012, the case was reopened, bringing hope and opportunity to actively participate in bringing about social change.

# PRET-A-

# PROTEST

KAMIST
IST

Lauren Gomez

# "Sextremists": FEMEN Protest!

In the waging of social wars and the execution of political revolt, no image or action is arbitrary. Fashion, via the body (both physical and politic) plays a particularly vital role in the sphere of global protest. Fashion marks persons as 'comrade' or 'enemy,' may serve as protector from natural environments and constructed weaponry or as canvas for the dissemination of dissent. Slogans, banners and graffiti have all been projected onto the human form, creating the idea of 'body as billboard.' Though the human body has been used as a canvas in both performance and protest alike,

> Theories of social movements by and large have been detached from the growing field of the sociology of the body. Although the human body is a vehicle of all social protest, analytical questions raised by the "protesting body" of men and women have been mostly neglected...[yet] studying the role of the acting body in social protest is critical to understanding the cultural outcomes and consequences of social movements (Taylor & Van Willigen 1996).

On August 30, 2012, members of feminist-activist group "CODE PINK" dressed up as giant vaginas made out of cloth, foam core, ribbon, chiffon and netting. They appeared at the Republican National Convention to protest what has been dubbed by the news media as "The War on Women," or the suppression of women's reproductive rights by Republican legislatives in Congress. Protestors held signs with slogans that read, "My Vagina, My Choice!" "Read my Lips: End War on Women" and "Can't Say It? Don't Legislate it!" at the convention in Tampa, Florida. One representative of the group commented,

> Today I hope to create a strong network of inspired and engaged activists. I want to make waves here in Tampa. I want the Republicans to see that there is dissent and that we're not going to stand for their rhetoric against women [as exemplified by] most recently, Representative Aiken making that comment about 'legitimate rape' and woman being able to control the situation as to whether or not they get pregnant...[it] is an outrage to women all over the country. When an interviewer for media group BuzzFeed asked her "And, why dress up?" She replied, simply, "To make a scene!" (Gauthler 2012)

Members of "Pussy Riot," a feminist, activist, art collective have also historically used dress as a tool for protest. Pussy Riot is defined on their website as, "an anonymous Russian feminist performance art group formed in October 2011." (FreePussyRight.org) On their site, the group describes their work as "peaceful performances in highly visible places" that is interested in "expressing the values and principles of gender equality, democracy and freedom of expression contained in the Russian constitution and other international instruments, including the Universal Declaration of Human Rights and the CEDAQ Convention." (FreePussyRiot.org)

Two members of Pussy riot are currently incarcerated (a third was recently released), for their "Punk Rock Prayer" which was performed at the Cathedral of Christ the Savior in Moscow on February 21st of this year. During this prayer of protest, Nadezhda Tolokonnikova, Maria Alyokhina and Yekaterina Samutsevich donned brightly colored tights, dresses and knitted baklavahs as they moshed on the alter, yelling, "Virgin Mary, Mother of God, banish [Putin], we pray thee!" (Rumens 2012)

James Brooke, for Women News Network, reports:

> Coming from Eastern Europe, Ukraine's Femen and Russia's Pussy Riot band represent a new kind of feminist protest, theatrical and radical. In Kiev, activists train regularly for protests. Behind the training is anger that Eastern European women are 30 years behind Western European women, in salaries and in job discrimination by employers. "They say, 'You will get married in a few years, or even like, in a few months you will be pregnant, like you are not a good worker, I don't want to have you in my office," Shevchenko says. "Or, like the second way to work there, they say that you have to sleep with me, we have to have sex. And we can do nothing."(Brooke 2012)

## FEMEN: An Introduction

FEMEN is a 'radical' feminist Ukrainian protest group based in Kiev, founded by long-time activist Anna Hutsol in 2008. The members of FEMEN are self-named "sextremists" and, according to their website, "are morally and physically fit soldiers, who every day make civil actions of the high[est] degree of difficulty and provocativity." (Femen.org)

Inna Shevchenko, FEMEN's current leader, asserts members of FEMEN need not necessarily be female, but most of its activists are. So, for the most part, the term 'FEMEN' describes an international group of young activist women who use their bodies as signs upon which to ascribe their words of dissent. Members photographed and portrayed in film footage are most often young, physically fit and topless. The group's site describes FEMEN as "the founder of a new wave of feminism of the third millennium [which has] followers all over the world."

The fact that most members of FEMEN look like Spice Girls and Pageant Queens is no accident. The current leader of FEMEN, Inna Shevchenko, explained at "The Truth is Concrete" Conference in April 2012, that it is not that all members of FEMEN who are young, fit, beautiful---and well, blonde. Instead, she asserts that those are the women photographed by the media; those are the activists who capture the attention of the lens. So, the collective, in turn, has come to be defined by one hyper-fashioned image: an Eastern European woman with long flowing hair and the (half naked) body of a swimsuit model.

## Framing FEMEN in "The Women Economy"

The Ukraine is a nation of muddled sexual politics. According to Larysa Kobelianska, head of a United Nations-led women's rights program, on average women in the Ukraine earn 30% less than men for equal work, and many remain unemployed. She also reports, "women make up only 8.5 percent of the Ukrainian parliament compared with an average of 30 percent in Europe." Additionally, "Prime Minister Mykola Azarov named an all-male Cabinet... [in 2010] saying 'conducting reforms is not a woman's business.' "And, while a female Prime Minister, Yulia Tymoshenko, did serve in the Ukraine, she was removed from office on potentially false charges. It should be noted that Tymoshenko then engaged in a protest of her own, going on a hunger strike for nearly a month in opposition to the charges that—perhaps prematurely—removed her from office. (The Moscow Times 2010)

The industries of sex trafficking — "it is estimated that 420,000 women have been trafficked out of the country in the last few years alone"—and Mail-Order Brides, or "Marriage Agencies," still fuel the nations economy (Clappeart 2012). The Ukraine is also the home of what Forbes Magazine is now calling 'The Barbie Flu.' Valeria Lukyanova, now known as the 'life-size Barbie' and 'Anime girl," Anastasiya Shpagina are just two of a series of Ukrainian women who are transforming themselves into life-sized dolls. Lukyanova and Shpagina have garnered international media attention for the body-modification they've endured to meet a 'plastic' ideal. Lukyanova has physically transformed herself to look like Mattel's iconic figuring, while

Shpagina has altered her face and body to look like a real-life Anime or Manga character.

In a society in which women are often unwillingly used as currency in the sex trade, while others still are consciously exploiting their bodies for media attention and cyber-'stardom,' where is feminism? And is there a place for it?

In April of 2012, Shevchenko gave a lecture at the "Truth is Concrete" Conference, a gathering described as "a 24/7 marathon camp on artistic strategies in politics and political strategies in art (Source: Truthisconcrete.org)." She states that feminism did not exist in the Ukraine before the emergence of FEMEN. The group's site describes FEMEN as "the founder of a new wave of feminism of the third millennium [which has] followers all over the world. The symbol of the organization [is] a wreath of flowers that adorns the head of bold women on all five continents." (Femen.org)

On the other hand, FEMEN founder Anna Hutsol told Natalia Antonova of Moscow News,

> We use eroticism in our approach and our dress. That's not sanctioned by feminism. People sneer at us all the time: 'You're against the sex industry, but you are all dressing like sex-workers'. But Ukrainian sex workers by and large don't own their own bodies. That's not how it works with us. When one of our girls went topless on Independence Square, she was doing it as a radical act. And it gets people talking. (Women News Network 2012)

## The Spectacle of Body as Billboard

The members of FEMEN, whose reach seems to span the world, are often described on the web, in link descriptions and video headlines, as "topless protesters." But whether or not this categorization is too reductive remains to be seen.

Much of the literature describing the work and aims of FEMEN, or, that which is accessible from the United States, exists in the form of YouTube videos. In a video called, "Who are FEMEN?" created by FEMEN members and posted on YouTube under the category "Nonprofits and Activism," a member describes the mission of the collective. A voiceover (in English) translates the woman's words (originally Ukranian).

The FEMEN representative says, "Hi, we are the women's movement FEMEN, we fight against sex for sale and freedom of sexual behavior. We express our ideas in flamboyant and shocking street actions. We are the coolest in Europe. Don't believe it? LET'S GO!" The video then pans over to protests including mud-wrestling fights (in which two women, scantily clad and covered in mud, kiss before the camera), women in bikinis and stilettos covering each other in bubbles in a public fountain, and a performance reenacting a rape scene.

Is the work of FEMEN nothing more than pornographic political propaganda? How do we reconcile the use of bodies—more specifically, women's bodies— in the pursuit of a political agenda? Is self-objectification somehow more just than the commodification of the body by 'the other?' Inna Shevchenko, in an interview with Eleanor Beardsley of NPR Europe, says, "whether it's Paris or Kiev, women share a common cause, fighting against patriarchy and all of its manifestations: religion, the sex industry, dictatorship." She speaks of "peaceful terrorism," in which the members of FEMEN are able to affront their 'enemies' without fear or violence, employing the power of their bodies. Beardsley goes on to report,

> Shevchenko has demonstrated for women's causes for years. But she says it was only when they began doing it topless that people paid attention. "In a protest like that I see a great potential of women's nudity [being used] as a weapon. And I understand every time, more and more, that it works. That it is a peaceful way," Shevchenko says. 'But they are even ready to use violence against our peaceful, naked bodies. " (Beardsley 2012)

Devon Novotnak

# Solidarity Shawls: Strategic Dress by the Mothers of the Plaza de Mayo

Social movements and dress are two ideas that are rarely ever included in the same conversation. Yet for the Mothers of the Plaza de Mayo in Argentina, dress became a crucial tactic in employing symbolism in their strategic nonviolent action. For these women, the white shawl draped around their head as they silently protested at the Plaza de Mayo became a critical way in employing symbolism and protesting the state of their disappeared children by the military junta in power. After years of military conflict and subversive activity by rebel groups during the Dirty War period from 1976 - 1983, the junta decimated the young adult generation by systematically 'disappearing' any individuals who were deemed a threat to the military government in power. In this sense 'disappearing' refers to the kidnapping, killing, and general removing of individuals from society with no known whereabouts for the family left behind. For these women, the white shawl was not just a signifier of the political and social movement of the Mothers, but of their familial role as well, one that had been intimately affected by the actions of the military junta. As political scientist Marguerite Guzman Bouvard stated within her work "Revolutionizing Motherhood":

> In adopting the baby shawls as their insignia the Mothers embarked on the use of powerful symbols that would not only identify them but that would also represent a reality in stark contrast to the brutality of the military regime. The shawls symbolized peace, life, and maternal ties, and they represented the claim of family bonds and ethical values in the public arena. (Guzman Bouvard 1994: 75)

The dress practices of the Mothers of the Plaza de Mayo, specifically through their use of the white shawl, demonstrates the critical connection between dress and social justice and movements. By examining the ways in which feminist theory examines social justice, we can effectively look at the way dress is employed by women as a tactic for justice.

According to feminist theorists Carol Gilligan and Grace Clement, there are two perspectives on social justice, a masculine ethic of justice and a feminine ethic of care. The ethic of justice relates to the rational, more formal perspective on law. Alternatively, theorists note that,

> The ethic of care, however, assumes relational factors – that is, attachment, connectedness, relations, context – as most important; in other words, the interactional dynamics of specific human beings in contextualized settings are prioritized. This is most often found in family and friendship settings. The assumption in the ethics of care model is that the self is socially constituted in its ongoing relationships with various others. (Capeheart & Milovanovic 2007: 23)

Thus, when considering social justice from a feminist perspective, the family and social relationships become integral to considering notions of justice. Clement also notes that the masculine ethic of justice should be considered in tangent with the ethic of care. Both ethics, she notes, "...must remain in the oscillating state for more genuine justice to take place" (Capeheart & Milovanovic 2007: 22). Thus, when examining the Mothers of the Plaza de Mayo, we could consider their pursuit of social justice from the perspective of the ethic of care, which provides a framework through which the women within this organization act upon the basis of relationships and familial bonds.

## The Dirty War

An examination of the actions of the Mothers of the Plaza de Mayo requires a context of the uneasy state of Argentina at the time. The 1970's marked great economic, political, and social strife for the Argentinean people. In 1976, President Isabel Peron was successfully overthrown by top generals in a coup that reinstated a new military dictatorship. The history of coups and military rule left the junta with a legacy "...in preserving the moral and ideological health of the nation as well as the concept of the enemy as internal" (Guzman Bouvard 1994: 20). While the military carried out strikes against guerilla groups such as the People's Revolutionary Army and the Montoneros, there was another layer to their campaigns that hit closer to home. In these cases, any individual that was deemed 'dangerous' to the government was met with decisive force from the military regime, including students, educators, and intellectuals. What was considered subversive was not just limited to these prominent guerrilla groups. As a result, the actions carried out by the military's special forces resulted in thousands of disappearances and little answers to the fate of a large part of the young adult generation. Thus, this time period in Argentina, from 1976 to 1983, is now known as the Dirty War.

## The Mothers of the Plaza de Mayo

Those disappeared by the junta left behind family, friends, and other loved ones waiting for answers. From the confusion and fear instilled in the military, an unexpected group of women emerged to challenge authority and demand answers of the fate of their children. These women were the mothers of the students and activists who had disappeared. Not only did they not know whether their children were dead or alive, but they were met with denial and resistance from the junta. As a result, a group of mothers seeking answers about their disappeared loved ones became the Mothers of the Plaza de Mayo. What started as a few distressed women coming together for support and answers became a nationwide movement.

Yet in a largely patriarchal society, the Mothers had to work to be heard and especially be seen. The military complex of the Argentinean government reinforced masculine ideals and traditional feminine roles, especially the woman's role as a good mother. Additionally, Argentina, with a largely Hispanic-Catholic culture, was a historically more repressive environment for women (Taylor 2001: 205). In this case the Mothers were placed in a precarious situation. Social movements can incite strong emotion and reactionary violence. By engaging in strategic nonviolent action, groups can more effectively work towards their aims. As stated within the work "Women and Social Protest", "Expressive political action is often used not only as a tactic, but also as a way of releasing emotion when more direct protest is prohibited or consequences are dangerous" (West & Blumberg 1990: 28). Thus, the women quickly discovered that their action had to employ more creativity. One of the ways in which the women did this was through their dress, reinforcing symbolism of the mother imagery. The primary garment they used was the white shawl or kerchief, frequently used in Argentinean culture as a children's diaper. As sociologist Diane Taylor explains:

> They started wearing white head kerchiefs to recognize each other and to be recognized by onlookers. The mothers realized that only by being visible could they be politically effective. Only by being visible could they stay alive in a society in which all opposition was annihilated by the military. The role of "mother" offered the women a certain security in the initial phase of their movement. (Taylor 2001: 100)

As demonstrated by the Mothers, the white kerchief provided intense imagery and power for the marginalized group of women facing the military junta. As they discovered, this garment allowed them to reinforce the idea of the "good" mother that had been used against them. As Taylor further explains:

> The Mothers' performance of motherhood tried to bridge the schism between the "good" woman and the "bad" woman belaboured by the military. The women consciously modeled themselves on the Virgin Mary, the ultimate

> mother who transcends the public/private bind by carrying her privacy with her even in public. Thus, Christian and Jewish women alike initially played the Mater Dolorosa and exploited a system of representations and stereotypes that had so effectively limited most forms of female visibility and expression... (Taylor 2001: 102)

From a feminist perspective of social justice, the use of stereotypes of motherhood relies heavily on the tactics that enforce the ethic of care. The pure whiteness, reminiscent of innocent infants, and the valued role of mother and caregiver could not have been symbolically achieved without the use of the white shawl. Additionally, this imagery provides a point from which the private experience of motherhood within the home becomes a very real and public experience within the plaza.

## Justice for the Mothers

Considering the successful use of the white shawl as tactic and symbol within social justice, we must also consider the greater context of the movement of the Mothers of the Plaza de Mayo. Up until 2006 the Mothers still circled the plaza every Thursday afternoon in search for answers of the disappeared. While the number of the disappeared is still disputed between the Mothers, government, and human rights organizations, a great portion of these individuals are still missing. In fact, the effectiveness of the Mothers has often been debated when comparing the numbers and the effects of the Dirty War. Yet the Mothers, with their iconic imagery of the white shawl, brought international awareness to the disappeared in Argentina. Additionally, they provided a place and space for women's voice and action in social movements. Thus, in examining dress and social justice in the case of the Mothers of the Plaza de Mayo there is a clear relationship present in which dress and specific garments provided the necessary imagery for the Mothers to successfully engage the public symbol of the powerful, maternal figure and inspire the next wave of feminist social justice.

58%
DONT WANT
ERSHING

Cally Carbone

# Support a Cause, Wear a T-shirt

Dress itself can be considered a form of language: conveying messages, expressing feelings, and inciting critique. It is a sign system in which people relate to others and the world around them. Fashion theorist Patrizia Calefato discusses text, language in fashion in a chapter entitled "Dress, Language and Communication" in her book *The Clothed Body* (2004). "Like language in this sense, dress functions as a kind of 'syntax', according to a set of more or less constant rules...These rules allow a garment, and body coverings in general, to acquire meaning, whether that of a veritable social significance... or a pure and simple exhibition of interconnected signs on the body following associative criteria established by the fashion system" (Calefato 2004: 5). A large part of the established fashion language is based on styling of garments and color. What does it mean then, when garments are emblazoned with words?

The 1980s brought us clothing adorned with slogans for thought, new ideas or specific causes. Being heard through voice became no longer the only option, by wearing words on a shirt anyone could see the position of the wearer, speaking out for or against particular issues. The trend has continued into present day, especially with what appears to be nearly every charity and foundation producing t-shirts to support and promote the chosen cause. This case study intends to address the use and popularity of the t-shirt as a basis of sharing a message and awareness for social justice, bringing more than just fashion into discourse.

Fashion designer, Katharine Hamnett made her name in the industry by creating protest t-shirts, white t-shirts with large black lettering. The first protest t-shirts were launched in 1983. The initial sayings printed on the t-shirts were: CHOOSE LIFE, WORLDWIDE NUCLEAR BAN NOW, PRESERVE THE RAINFORESTS, SAVE THE WORLD, SAVE THE WHALES, EDUCATION NOT MISSILES. Hamnett's t-shirts were "designed to be copied, with the objective of effecting change by being seminal, using the excess media coverage that the label was receiving. T-shirts sold with a percentage going to charity" (Katharine Hamnett n.d). Then in 1984, Hamnett famously wore one of her creations to meet then Prime Minister of the United Kingdom, Margaret Thatcher, an oversized white t-shirt with '58% DON'T WANT PERSHING' printed on the front in large black letters. The shirt was in reference to British public's distaste of the Prime Minister's decision to allow Pershing missiles from the United States to be kept in Great Britain (Arthur 2012). According to Hamnett in an article in The Times, she did not show up wearing the protest t-shirt, but she smuggled it in with her and changed once inside the event the Prime Minister was hosting. Upon reading the message, Hamnett recounted that Thatcher shrieked and quickly quipped, "Oh, we haven't got Pershing here. So maybe you're at the wrong party" (Olins 2008). No matter the political happenstance, Hamnett's intention was clear and after years, now infamous.

Hamnett continued to create t-shirts with protest-style messages after her iconic publicity stunt. "To this day my slogan t-shirts are copied, worn and reiterated. From a fashion perspective it's flattering. From a political perspective, it's exactly what I set out to achieve - to sow seeds of change and help people create a voice" (Katharine Hamnett (n.d). And it is not necessarily copying that has extended Hamnett's reputation, but she herself launched new collections of protest t-shirts. Most recently in Spring 2012, Hamnett partnered with H&M for Britain's Climate Week. Hamnett, an avid supporter of the Environmental Justice Foundation and campaigner for ethical and environmental cotton, produced a t-shirt for the event that said SAVE THE FUTURE. The t-shirt retailed for £9.99, was sold only at select H&M stores, made from 100% organic cotton, and was made with renewable energy (Grazia (2012). The price point of her H&M t-shirts were a fraction of the cost of her mainline t-shirts that retail for £69.00, even with the same message. A further critique could be made to discuss the implications of organic cotton and renewable energy made t-shirts at such a low price.

To analyze Hamnett's political perspective ambition, it is worthwhile to start with a summarized view of theorist John Rawls concepts of justice, particularly "natural rights belonging to all individuals" (Tai 2009: 454) and those natural rights including the liberty of speech, among others such as assembly and private property. Rawls expanded his notions to formulate the model veil of ignorance; which establishes the hypothetical scenario that people would not know the societal status they will eventually end up with at birth (Tai 2009). "What the veil of ignorance scenario assures is that in setting up policy, everyone would be considering and looking out for everyone else in society" (Tai 2009: 455).

With Hamnett's t-shirts, it is first the freedom of speech that determinable and understood. By wearing the t-shirt, the person is not only embodying the physical garment, but the idea and purpose of the written statement printed on the t-shirt, sharing with anyone viewing, the principles the wearer stands for. Even though the words are not spoken, it is still a form of speech. Secondly, the statement or slogan is obviously a social distributive justice message, in most instances, and especially in the case of Katharine Hamnett's t-shirts, the significance is for the majority of everyone in society, just as the concern through the veil of ignorance. Her SAVE THE FUTURE campaign can be interpreted many ways, but no matter what, it is justifiably for the masses. Hamnett addresses the topic of her t-shirt with The Ecologist, sharing her thoughts:

> I mean there's not much time left to do it. I think the t-shirts...you can't not read them. There's no way that you can look at someone and not read what it says. It passes all the filters, gets into your brain and makes you think and actually take some positive action. If we care about extinction of species, if we care about life on earth, if we care about survival of the human race, if we care about a habitable planet, we just have to adjust our lifestyle. The slightest change would have an enormous impact. If we all tried to buy organic cotton whenever we could, if that would be our first choice in cotton garments, it would have an enormous impact. (Styles 2012)

Hamnett's primary goal was and still is to provoke change and create awareness to a problem that is experienced by society, through the visual nature of her t-shirts. Earl Tai offers a distributive justice approach to observing the designed visual as an important part of our cultural exchange and "the increasing awareness of and co-option of the sociopolitical power of our visual and material world for political agendas" (2009: 456).

To further illustrate Tai's view, there are multiple t-shirts that could be analyzed, as the practice to support a charity or diplomatic reason is currently a very popular action for support and awareness. Most of such t-shirts, like Katharine Hamnett's, go beyond the printed message and a portion of the proceeds go toward the stated cause. While the options are seemingly limitless, let the following examples be an offering for additional representation.

The first t-shirt for this continued exploration is from 2010 and was a response to a catastrophic event that took place in the small island nation of Haiti. The Council for Fashion Designers of America released a t-shirt project to help contribute to the Clinton Bush Haiti Fund that went help support efforts after the country was devastated by an earthquake. The t-shirt read TO HAITI WITH LOVE primarily, and in smaller text HOPE HELP HEAL HAITI (Clements 2010). The project went even farther to gain media attention by enlisting a celebrity spokesperson, Beyoncé. Through promotion of the t-shirt, she called for action, "Join me and the fashion industry by buying and wearing the Fashion for Haiti T-shirt. Together we can send a message of hope by raising much-needed funds for the people of Haiti" (Ibid). The specificity of the message, singled out a population less fortunate than most, stricken by an unfortunate natural disaster; and the t-shirt was created for donation purposes and for the wearer to share with anyone who viewed, their support for a cause. But one must ask, who is being seen or heard from through the t-shirt, the celebrities supporting the cause, such as Beyoncé, or the struggling people of Haiti?

The second t-shirt chosen for this study, is the one popularized by the charity Stand Up to Cancer. Founded in 2008, the charity gained popularity more recently by running television advertisements with major credit card company, MasterCard, and partnering with Major League Baseball. The charity seeks to accelerate cancer research, to fund new therapies, so cancer patients' lives are saved quickly. Stand Up to Cancer's catchphrase: "This is where the end of cancer begins: when we unite in one movement, unstoppable (Stand Up To Cancer 2012). The charity and its partnerships are very far from the fashion industry as previous examples have been, in most immediate instances, but what they do have are t-shirts, and recognizable ones at that. The sale of the t-shirts goes directly to the charity's funds. By wearing the t-shirt, it does not matter if the wearer has cancer, knows someone with or who had cancer, or lost someone to cancer, the message is that they are a supporter of cancer research. Their investment in the t-shirt is going toward social awareness for those afflicted by a disease that affects a majority of the population. Cancer does not choose people because of their status, even more of an argument for enacting distributive justice through the visual.

When we introduce social justice t-shirts into our wardrobes; we no longer wear our heart on our sleeve, but undoubtedly front and center.

TO
WITH
LOVE
HELP HEAL HAITI

HAND
OFF MY
VAGINA

Devon Novotnak

# Codepink: Power, Peace, and Pink Dresses

At the 2012 Republican National Conference, the women's peace group Codepink displayed one of the most provocative and certainly one of the 'pinkest' protests in response to the Republican 'War on Women'. Dressed as vaginas, the women of Code Pink displayed signs readings "Read my lips. End War on women." And "Hands off my vagina." (Bond 2012). In solidarity, they confronted the Republican Party through the use of visual imagery to reclaim rights over their own bodies. Since the beginning of Codepink in 2002, the activist group has used visual forms of protest such as this one to convey their message about ending the war and stopping the next war to the American people. At first, Codepink had solely addressed the injustice of war and the affects on women and families internationally. Yet the organization has extended beyond war to address issues ranging from women's rights and who has control over women's bodies, to drone activity and the targeting of civilians in Pakistan. Thus, Codepink targets a range of injustices internationally and within the United States by using humor and creativity, especially through costume, to reach their audience and effectively spread their message. These values and tactics helped form a solid identity and recognizable tactics for the group. As described in the publication, *Stop the Next War Now: Effective Responses to Violence and Terrorism*, edited by Code Pink founders Medea Benjamin and Jodie Evans,

> The imagination and creativity of many women, woven together, became CODEPINK: Women for Peace. Determined to stop the invasion of Iraq, we threw our hearts and souls into that effort ... We draped forty-foot pink slips (in the shape of women's lingerie) off rooftops to all for the firing of the armchair warriors. We brought pink badges of courage to the lonely truth tellers who advocated peace. (Benjamin & Evans 2005: xv)

Thus through the use of signature pink and creativity through costume and display, Codepink challenges gender stereotypes and claims spaces of power in the field of strategic nonviolent action. Additionally, this very act raises a paradox in the injustice of women's relationship to dress. While fashion is seen as traditionally feminine it is not necessarily associated with the power of women. Codepink attempts to subvert these ideas through their use of dress. A better way to understand the actions of Codepink and the creative use of dress is through the literature on social justice that can then be applied to individual actions of protest by the organization.

Working through the lens of social justice, an appropriate way to view the actions of Codepink, especially in reference to their dress, is through the feminist ethic of care. According to Loretta Capeheart and Dragan Milovanovic in their work *Social Justice: Theories, Issues, and Movements,* the feminist ethic of care within social justice states that, "Formal equality before the law overlooks the factor that the male notion of justice is incorporated in discussions of what is just, and female notions are relegated to subordinate positions" (Capeheart and Milovanovic 2007: 22). The authors continue to include the work of theorists such as Carol Gilligan and Grace Clement who have accounted for a familial and relationship based form of justice. This framework for looking at social justice is incredibly important when looking at the work of Code Pink. In their mission statement the organization states, "...Women have been the guardians of life – not because we are better or purer or more innately nurturing than men, but because men have busies themselves making war" (Benjamin & Evans 2005: 233). In this sense, a militaristic sense of justice has resulted from a masculine control of power. Subsequently, the voices of mothers, daughters, sisters, and wives have become subordinate to the current state of war. These foundations of justice are based more so on the relationship, thus in tangent with the feminist ethic of care.

Why then, is it critical to understand a feminist notion of social justice when looking at the dress practices of Code Pink? Mainly, the answer lies within the exacerbation of gender stereotypes in costume that members use to reclaim power and draw attention through irony and humor. The way in which we can look more closely at this idea is to focus specifically on what is worn within Code Pink and how it is incorporated as an organization. As sociologist Rachel Kutz-Flamenbaum notes within her own ethnography on the demonstrates by the group:

> It is a sea of pink. Every shade, every form, lots and lots of pink everywhere. The people who stand out in this crowd are those who are not wearing pink. In order to help people dress in pink, to the left of the stage there were bags of pink thrift store clothes free for the taking. Several people I talked to over the past two days referred to going to thrift stores to get pink clothes to be part of Code Pink. Code Pink volunteers were also selling pink buttons, pink silk scarves parasols and hats and t-shirts. (Kutz-Flamenbaum 2003: 94)

Initially from this description we notice the symbolic power of the color pink in this context. Pink remains stereotypically feminine, yet in gross amounts it establishes a female solidarity. Power is established in the masses and in this case pink means power. Additionally, the accessibility to participate in this form of action should be noted. Pink does not become a solely inclusive color and through the act of recycling thrift store clothes, anyone who wants to participate can. Yet the women do not simply wear just pink, they embrace it. The women (and men) don pink in all shades, but notably have adopted hot pink in all its vibrancy. They also take the liberty to fully dress up in fun and outrageous outfits. Tutus, feather boas, and other forms of costumes are seen throughout Code Pink's members. Take for example, the actions of one Code Pink chapter in Texas and the way they utilized dress:

> ...During the final weeks of the 79th Texas Legislature, a group of women dressed in hot pink shirts, hats, wigs, and boas made their way through the capitol in Austin, delivering "pink slips" to offending legislators. Chanting "2, 4, 6, 8 high kicks can't impregnate," they draped a silky negligee on Representative Frank Edwards's (D-Houston) desk for his bill banning sexually suggestive cheerleading moves. (Pagani 2005)

The women did not just appear before the Legislature, but they performed as part of the spectacle of their protest. With their clothing going beyond the symbol of pink to pieces associated with costume and play, the women further exaggerate ideas of creativity and femininity.

Aside from these general acts of protest and solidarity, Code Pink performs specific, more intentional acts using costume. For instance, one of the first forms of protest they were noted for was the act of 'pink slipping' notable politicians and figures in power. The pink slip, while symbolic for the act of firing, actually was represented by a giant piece of women's lingerie or slip. On this giant, pink slip they would write, for example, "Dick's in bed with Halliburton, but we got screwed. Cheney you're fired." (Featherstone 2004: 11). The slip would then be hung on the side of a building as public display. The imagery and use of pun with women's lingerie again plays upon the gender stereotypes inherently mocked as well as embraced by Code Pink. Lingerie, a highly private item, also becomes an extremely public message that not only becomes visible, but reclaims power by symbolically firing politicians and government officials.

Another more recent act of protest occurred at the 2012 Republican National Convention. While many organizations publicly protest the GOP at the convention, Code Pink's recent actions reached national headlines. Going beyond the pink costume, the members appeared in homemade vagina costumes. With the costumes they had signs that said: "Read my lips. End war on women.", "Hands off my Vagina" and "Read my lips. Leave my vagina alone" (Bond 2012). The women used blunt terminology and their graphic costumes to call attention to what they call, the 'war on women' being waged by the Republican Party. What some may have seen as offensive they used as a tool to garner attention to the issues women are facing within the election. Additionally, this use of dress references issues occurring within politics around the use of the actual word 'vagina' again in a humorous way. As co-founder Medea Benjamin said,

> I've never seen police smile so much when we go by, a bunch of marching vaginas. It's been very positive, there are a number of women in the Republican party that want to come up to us and talk about it. And we remind them of what happened to Lisa Brown when she, an elected official in Michigan who said the word 'vagina' on the floor and was banished and couldn't speak for another week. So we tell them if you can't say the word then don't legislate it. (Domenighini 2012).

As Benjamin emphasizes, positivity is key to the demonstrations Code Pink participates in. While the messages they are conveying are serious in nature, they approach it through humor and creativity, which the costumes, such as the vaginas, provide.

Ultimately, Code Pink's use of dress is key to understanding contemporary notions of feminine acts of social justice. Through an understanding of a feminist ethics of care we can better appreciate the position women's peace groups, especially Code Pink, are approaching from. Dress practices provide an incredibly important source of power for these women in their subversion of gender stereotypes and use of human and creativity. In appreciating the relationship between dress and Code Pink we may look beyond the striking color and unapologetic imagery to a deeper connection between gender, power, and dress.

Yes We Can
End War!

# THE PARADOX

# OF AID

DaMarkis Brown

# "One for One": Problems or Solutions?

TOMS is a name that has become synonymous with both style and social activism. Since its inauguration in 2006, the company has gained the support from many social activist and fashionistas alike. TOMS shoes was founded by reality-tv star, Blake Mycoskie, who was motivated by a disease, that many people in developing countries face, known as podoconiosis. Podoconiosis is caused from walking in silica-rich soil and can cause the feet to swell and also causes other health issues (Sharaby 2009). When Mycoskie noticed how many young children were faced with the disease he took action by starting his company, which he stated would create an longer last impact, opposed to simply starting a charity and handing out money. Blake then created a mission statement, which set his company apart from many other sustainable brands, that states that the company would match every pair of new shoes purchased with a pair of new shoes to give to a child in need. This movement became known to many as the "One for One" movement.

On the TOMS Shoes website, they point out that to date they have issued "over 2 million shoes to children in need around the world". They also explain why shoes are so important to children in these undeveloped areas. In addition to the possible chance of being infected with the Podoconiosis disease, children also have a higher chance of getting cuts and sores on their feet. These cuts and sores could also become infected without protection from shoes thus, creating further health complications. One of the last reasons listed for the need for shoes was because of the need for completed school uniforms. The website states:

> Many times children can't attend school barefoot because shoes are a required part of their uniform. If they don't have shoes, they don't go to school. If they don't receive an education, they don't have the opportunity to realize their potential.

This statement is interesting, considering that education is valued in every country. Yet, some countries create an injustice to the families by requiring additional financial necessities. It is evident that the idea of children being gifted a pair of shoes is a blessing because it not only prevents them from unsafe conditions but it allows them to obtain an education. In this way, the company is giving children from these various countries the opportunity to live a "normal child's life" similar to children from developed countries.

Blake's initiative to give back to those who are less fortunate are surely recognized with his "one for one" movement, however the for-profit company could easily be recognized as just another participant of this country's infamous capitalism. Mycoskie comes from a wealthy background that allowed him to take vacations to Argentina, hence the motivation behind his shoes. He based his idea on the Espadrille shoe which he noticed many Argentinian farmers wearing during his visit. One could assume that the espadrille shoe is not only inexpensive, as many of the farmers owned them, but also inexpensive to make. So this brings up the question of why are TOMS shoes so expensive if they are essentially the same shoe that is being worn in these undeveloped countries. TOMS are sold in stores like Neiman Marcus for up to $80, a price that the average American could possible be opposed to paying for shoes.

This would not be so questionable if the children in these various countries were receiving the same type of shoe as American's were, opposed to the very basic and inexpensive looking TOMS shown on the website. It seems as though TOMS has reaped the benefits of their clever marketing, in which they position their company as a charity opposed to a profit earning company. Any American who is socially and environmentally conscious would be eager to participate in such a movement because they are being involved in several positive actions. They are giving back to undeveloped countries, practicing sustainability by using eco-friendly products and looking stylish all simultaneously. However many people are not seeing the bigger problem that a company like this is creating. TOMS is creating a short term solution opposed to a long lasting change in the problems that these Argentinian communities are facing as charity is not the same as justice. For one, these espadrilles are made of extremely loose materials. Even American consumers often find that the shoes are not durable. What happens when these children's shoes are worn and no longer wearable? Will they simply be given another pair?

Also, the act of giving is in itself very problematic. It undercuts any type of market that is already established and creates a sense of dependence on the free donations. If TOMS truly wants to help these countries wouldn't it be more beneficial to work directly with local craftsmen and merchants to produce and distribute the shoes, which would in-turn build that country's economy? This could also directly impact the environment by cutting on shipping and packing cost and sourcing of local materials, only further benefiting these countries. Although TOMS is a good attempt at helping others, we must question whether Blake is really helping them? It seems like we, as consumers and supporters of the brand, are merely promoting dependence, as suggested by philosopher Slavoj Zizek in his lecture *First as Tragedy, Then as Farce* (2009), and further contributing to our capitalist economy.

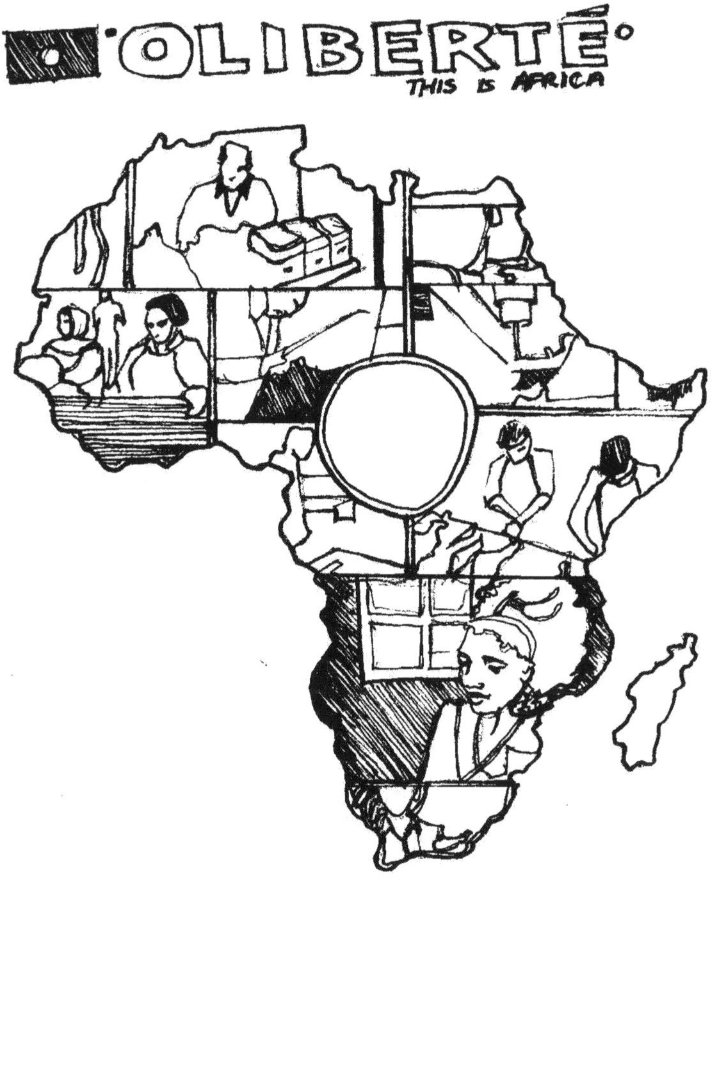
OLIBERTÉ
THIS IS AFRICA

Gisela Aguilar

# Oliberté Breaks the Charity Chains

If you were asked to think about African fashion would the words "hip," "stylish," or "premium quality" come to mind? For Tal Dehtiar, his goal is to make consumers and manufacturers alike associate those aforementioned adjectives with the fashion consumer goods coming out of Africa. Dehtiar, a 30-something year old Canadian, who started and sold his non-profit organization MBAs Without Borders, was inspired by his voyages and his desire to change the philosophical formula of most "fashion for a cause" brands. In 2009, he founded Oliberté ("liberté" meaning freedom in French, "O" taken from his national anthem), which he describes as "the first company to make premium shoes in Africa using African materials and explicitly linking shoes sold by Western retailers to job creation on the continent" (Good.is 2011). Oliberté is a casual, hip, moderately priced fashion brand which started out selling leather shoes and has since branched out into leather bags and accessories. Dehtiar's company prides itself in delivering premium quality products through ethically and environmentally friendly means, but above all Oliberté strives to be the catalyst for the flourishing and thriving of Africa's middle class through employment opportunities at the company's factories (Oliberte 2012).

Dehtiar's ultimate goal is to reconceptualize the global perception of Africa, what it stands for, who its citizens are, and what the country is capable of, in order to do away with this "Third World" stigma. However, in order to dispel these stereotypical images of the African continent, Dehtiar argues that Africa must learn to sustain itself. Oliberté's mission statement asserts that one of its goals is "to support the growing middle class by building a world class footwear brand that can create thousands of jobs and encourages manufacturers from other industries to work in Africa" (Oliberte 2012: "Why Africa?"). Dehtiar stresses the importance of producing and selling premium quality merchandise made exclusively in Africa by Africans. Oliberté stitches and assembles its shoes in Ethopia, sourcing leather from local free-range, hormone-injection free cows, sheep, and goats. The shoes "crepe rubber soles" are made from the natural rubber of Liberian rubber trees, the leather bags and accessories sourced in Kenya and made in Zambia, and lastly the woven labels are produced in Mauritius (Oliberte 2012, "Why Africa?"). In 2009, Oliberté sold 200 shoes and this year projected sales are expected to reach between 20,000 and 25,000, according to a CNN profile on the Dehtiar's company (CNN 2011). Sales figures keep rising amidst a bevy of competing "socially-conscious fashion brands," yet Dehtiar is not deterred because of his company's unique approach towards its socially just cause.

The media has often referred to Oliberté as the "anti-TOMS" namely because of Dehtiar's priority to instill in his African employees a sense of personal and economic independence rather than base its social responsibility on charitable donations as many "socially-conscious" companies do (Hollender 2012). In an online interview, Dehtiar has stated that he considers TOMS to be a successful marketing tool but Oliberté is founded on the firm belief that "Africa can compete on a global scale [...] but it needs a chance. It doesn't need handouts or a hand up. It needs people to start shaking hands and companies to start making deals to work in these countries" (Good.is 2012).

As the philosopher Slavoj Zižek has pointed out, the charitable tactics such as the "one-for-one model" implemented by companies such as TOMS, where a pair of shoes is donated for every pair that is purchased, is inherently detrimental in that it perpetuates a foreign dependency, and prolongates a submissive position between impoverished countries and their "rescuers" (Zižek 2009). Oliberté's approach to ethical fashion and social justice takes on, what I would argue, the "human development approach" devised by the economic scholar Amartya Sen. As Sen states, this specific perspective of justice focuses on "making do with what we can [...] without expecting that this strategy will solve every decisional problem we face" (Sen 2008: 340). Through the perspective of a human development approach, Oliberté may be said to concentrate on the "importance of looking at human lives themselves, rather than at the commodity possessions [...] that have some influence over [their] lives," whereas a brand like TOMS appeals to a more immediate impact on the lives of individuals through its distribution of shoes to impoverished regions (Sen 2008: 334). Sen introduces this notion of seeing justice through a comparative perspective as a way to branch from pre-existing conceptions of justice which tend to dwell on speculating about the ideal just society and what it consists or does not consist of, whereas the comparative perspective finds ways for a society to be more just through taking action. Oliberté acts for justice through its mission to provide African citizens with opportunities for self-advancement and self-actualization through the means of employment (Sen 2008: 336f).

According to ethics scholar John Alexander "social justice consists in creating the greatest possible condition for the realization of basic capabilities for all" (Alexander 2008: 1). It is precisely the capabilities of the struggling community that Oblierté wishes to cultivate. Sen's understanding of justice can be particularly applicable to Obliberté's philosophy as "Sen advocates that people's well-being and standing in society should be evaluated on the basis of their 'capability to achieve valuable functionings'" (Alexander 2008: 56). "Functionings," as Sen would describe, are what an individual can achieve, whether it be acquiring education, maintaining health, or obtaining social recognition or self-respect. Dehtiar and his company attempt to provide all of these important elements of well-being through their ethically run company which provides "benefits like subsidized or free lunches," maternity leave, and is currently working on implementing programs like "health and life insurance, credit savings programs, and training" (Oliberte 2012, "Play Fair"). The capability theorist Elizabeth Anderson elaborates on issues of distribution of resources through "equal recognition" where justice is acted out by through a distribution founded on "principles and procedures that express respect and dignity" (Alexander 2008: 68). She goes onto say that we must be conscious of "avoiding a condescending attitude in coming in to the aid of people," something that Dehtiar vehemently eschews as he has stated that he "doesn't want Africa to be known for its cheap labor, or to feel pity on Africa" and instead wants Africa to be recognized as a center of commerce known for its high quality products (Alexander 2008: 68).

Oliberté has been recognized for addressing Africa's bottom line issues of poverty and lack of employment opportunities through its social justice philosophy and its "play fair" organizational attitude as a way to foster and stabilize a growing middle class. Yet it is too early to know for sure how exactly Oliberté has impacted Africa's global and local economic status. On the Oliberté website, Dehtiar acknowledges that there is certainly room for improvements, amongst them ecological challenges that the company must contend with such as their current need to fly out all their product to each African country where they manufactured (Oliberte 2012 "Environment). Additionally, we must also think of who is excluded in consuming Oliberté products as their leather shoes are priced anywhere from $120-185. Therefore, as consumers there is only a small percentage that can participate in this socially just endeavor. Although the higher prices may reflect the quality and labor required to produce them, and do cater to a certain economic market, Oliberté's lack of a "one-for-one" model may be a step in the right direction for socially aware fashion brands. It is this emphasis on capabilities that will enable impoverished countries like Africa to do away with the dependency that is proliferated by charity-oriented organizations.

FEED
THE CHILDREN OF
THE WORLD

# FEED Projects Turns Grocery Sacks into It-bags

According to their website, FEED began in 2006 when acclaimed model and activist Lauren Bush Lauren designed a bag to benefit the United Nations World Food Programme's School Feeding program (WFP). Lauren desired to use her love of fashion as a means of fundraising to right the wrong of child malnutrition and hunger around the globe. As a WFP Honorary Student Spokesperson, Lauren took a special interest in WFP's School Feeding program after visiting countries in Africa, Latin America, and Asia. The WFP School Feeding program feeds and educates hungry children in these places. Lauren then created the FEED 1 bag, a reversible burlap and organic cotton tote reminiscent of the bags of food distributed by WFP, to help raise funds and awareness around these school feeding operations. This first bag was stamped with "FEED the children of the world" and the number "1" to signify that each bag purchased feeds one child in school for a year. In 2007, FEED Projects LLC was founded by Lauren and Ellen Gustafson to produce and sell these bags. In addition to the company, FEED started a non-profit organization called the FEED Foundation, which supports programs and organizations that are effectively working to fight hunger and eliminate malnutrition throughout the world (FEED 2012).

The mission of FEED Projects is to create good products that help FEED the world. They do this through the sale of FEED bags, t-shirts, bears, and other accessories by building a set donation into the cost of each product. The impact of each product is signified by a stenciled number on the product, and is understandable, tangible, and meaningful (FEED: Our Mission 2012). In creating all FEED products, environmentally-friendly and artisan-made materials are used, along with fair-labor production. Ultimately, FEED believes that everyone has the right to basic human necessities, such as healthy and nutritious food. FEED asserts that they stand behind their brand and the organizations and humanitarian programs each FEED product supports, as "FEED is proud to help FEED the world, one bag at a time" (Feed: Our Mission 2012). FEED addresses the issue of hunger and malnutrition in the lives of children around the world, and seeks justice for this problem in a practical way by raising funds through the sale of fashionable consumer goods.

Since its formation, FEED Projects has partnered with many different brands and retailers to produce additional goods to be sold to support their cause. Partners include Whole Foods, Amazon.com, Rugby, Barnes & Noble, Disney, Bobbi Brown, Bloomingdales, Kenneth Cole, Bergdorf Goodman, Lord & Taylor, Pottery Barn, The GAP, Forever 21, HSN, American Eagle, and Clarins, among others (FEED: Timeline 2012). These collaborations resulted in an expansion of FEED Projects to support other causes such as literacy, healthy school eating in the United States, and natural disaster relief in Haiti and Japan. FEED Project's also expanded their product line to include additional styles of bags, smaller pouches, backpacks, bracelets, teddy bears, and t-shirts. Each item purchased contributes a particular number of school meals to their cause, or it contributes funds to one their extension projects. In 2010, FEED had their own pop-up shop on Fifth Avenue in New York City (FEED: Timeline 2012). Lauren has been featured in several fashion magazines discussing FEED, including Vogue and Lucky, and she herself is often photographed with FEED bags, such as the one she wore to the Met Ball last year.

The FEED bags themselves are modeled after the bags of food distributed by the WFP, and all FEED products are made from organic cotton, natural burlap, or recycled plastic-based nylon (FEED). Lauren states that some of the more expensive bags are handmade in Guatemala and Kenya by fair-labor organizations that employ local women, a small portion are made in the United States, while the bulk are made in China at a fair-trade factory that FEED Projects has audited by a third party (Fenn 2010). FEED's website explains where the money from FEED's products goes:

> Every FEED product has a specific and individual donation attached to the sale of the item. Rather than donating a "percentage of the profits or proceeds" like other organizations, we donate an actual amount of money from each product sold. The donation is built into the cost of the product - so it is an exact and tangible amount of money for each product. For example, for every purchase of the FEED 10 pouch, 10 school meals are provided to children. The donations from these 10 meals are then made by FEED to the UN World Food Programme (or our other partner organizations such as Room to Read, Millennium Villages, and the US Fund for UNICEF), based on the number of products sold to date at that time (FEED: FAQ's 2012).

The organization prides itself on being transparent, and allowing consumers to know exactly where the money they spend on FEED products goes. As a fashion good itself, the FEED bag is well-meaning, but somewhat disturbing.

It is a bag consumed by the wealthy that resembles a food bag for the poor. While it raises funds for the cause and awareness for the injustice occurring, the FEED bag's appropriation of the appearance of a food bag is inappropriate and unnecessary as it almost mocks the cause itself.

From a perspective of justice, this endeavor may possibly be seen as a successful way to raise money for a cause that clearly needs the funds, but it can also be seen as an encouragement to consume for charity's sake, and do so in a fairly cynical way. Philosopher Slavoj Zizek discusses the paradoxes of cultural capitalism and ethical consumerism, both which FEED Projects seemingly support (2009). We are not just buying a FEED bag, we are buying into the consumerist act, thus simultaneously undermining the social act of support. As Zizek would put it, we are buying into something bigger than a stylish burlap FEED bag, as we are at the same time fulfilling a series of ethical duties through a kind of "semantic over-investment" (Zizek 2009).

We are doing something to help starving children around the world. Clearly, helping starving children around the world is a noble and great thing, but doing so through the consuming of goods can be problematic as part of the origin of famines are created through the economic system. In today's society, as we consume, everything is included in this consumption; we buy a FEED bag and contribute to righting the wrong of world hunger at the same time. Lauren asserts that FEED Projects believes in "commerce with a purpose" (Raphael 2012). This becomes problematic when consumption replaces the act of actually working to solve the injustice. Consumption acts as a remedy that does not cure the disease, and can actually prolong it, or even make it worse (Zizek 2009). We feel justified in our consumptive practices because we believe it is contributing to the greater well-being of mankind, thus shying away from the corrupt system itself. We are encouraged to buy these goods, like FEED bags, but we are not encouraged to assist in reconstructing a broken system (Zizek 2009). We buy, and that is it; we have accomplished our part in working to solve injustice.

Economist Amartya Sen discusses the distinction between sympathy and commitment when it comes to the foundations for altruistic behavior. Sympathy "refers to one person's welfare being affected by the position of others" while commitment "is concerned with breaking the tight link between individual welfare (with or without sympathy) and the choice of ac tion" (Alexander 2008: 22). If people are moved only by sympathy, Sen states, then most other-regarding gestures (such as purchasing a FEED bag) can be explained in terms of self-interest (Alexander 2008: 22). In the sympathetic act of purchasing a FEED bag, people are asserting that they only care about others because it impacts their own welfare in some way. Buying and wearing a FEED bag allows you to show-off to others that you are concerned with justice, but only when you consequently gain from the contribution to the cause as well. When people are altruistic even if it goes against or minimizes their own welfare, that is commitment, and the purchase of a FEED bag does not encourage us to fight injustice by overriding one's own preferences (Alexander 2008: 22). Sen purports that it is commitment that brings people together for collective action in order to successfully right injustice (Alexander 2008, 23). Buying a FEED bag does not actually commit to solving injustice, but rather acts as sympathy for the cause, however noble that may be.

While their model of charitable consumption may be problematic, the actual contributions that FEED Projects is making to alleviate this injustice cannot be ignored or written off. As for the success of their mission and reducing the injustice that they purport, FEED is successful. From FEED's website we learn that to date, they have been able to raise enough money through the sale of products to provide over 60 million school meals to children around the world through WFP. Additionally, FEED has partnered with the United States Fund for The United Nations Children's Fund, raising funds for their Vitamin A and micronutrient supplements program to provide over 46,000 children with essential nutrients. Lauren states that FEED Project's success is based on how many children get fed, and that through their model the overwhelming issues of hunger and malnutrition are broken down to be made more meaningful and tangible for consumers (Garton 2011). Lauren states that when purchasing FEED products, consumers know exactly where their money is going and their exact donation to the cause. Furthermore, Lauren hopes that FEED's work can inspire everyone to get physically involved in the cause and fight injustice through more than just the purchase of FEED products (Raphael 2012).

Zizek asserts that "the real aim is to try and reconstruct society on such a basis that poverty will be impossible" (2009). In the case of FEED Projects, this would mean reconstructing society in a way that would alleviate the issues of child hunger. We must change who controls the resources and how these resources are distributed. FEED Projects is attempting to alleviate the immediate injustice of children not having enough food, while possibly working on a solution to the larger issue of shifting who controls the food in these poverty-stricken countries (Feed: Our Mission). FEED Projects recognizes that hunger is a complex issue "usually compounded by poverty, unemployment, lack of sanitation, food deserts, lack of education and resources, and overcrowding, among many other things" (FEED: Our Mission 2012). FEED's work with the United Nations World Food Programme and The United Nations Children's Fund assert the initiative's recognition that much is being done to fight world hunger and malnutrition in children, but that much is still left to be done to bring justice to light. Charitable consumption of fashion may reduce some injustices, though much remains to be done in reconstructing society so that these issues no longer exist.

WORLD FOOD
PROGRAMME
G NET

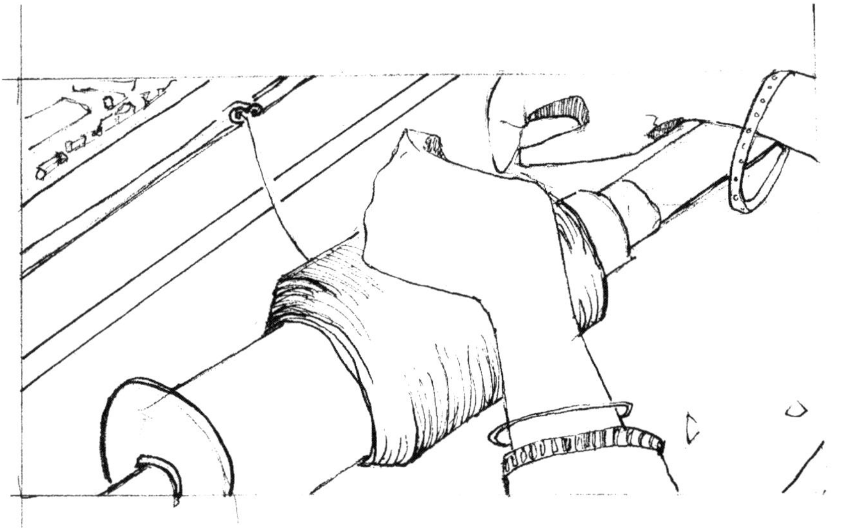

Devon Novotnak

# Beyond Economic Empowerment: Weaving Destination

For women who have been victims of sexual trafficking or are HIV positive, the opportunities to be economically sustainable or even accepted within their communities are few or do not exist. Within organizations such as Weaving Destination in North East India, the lack of opportunities for these disenfranchised women is seen as an injustice that fashion can help correct. Weaving Destination is a project of the Nedan Foundation and is also in collaboration with the United Nations Development Programme's (UNDP) Women and Wealth Project. This organization relies on the education of marketing, business, and traditional weaving skills within the modern fashion system of India to make locally produced goods. Additionally, Weaving Destination relies on workers who are vulnerable women who are HIV positive, have experienced human trafficking, or have been at risk for other gendered dangers within the region. By educating and offering these women this opportunity, Weaving Destination works to provide transferable skills and income that could benefit otherwise marginalized women in the long term. By examining this organization through the lens of social justice and the capabilities approach we may determine the usefulness of fashion in community development and empowerment.

Weaving Destination has been made possible by the Nedan Foundation. The Nedan Foundation is a non-governmental organization that focuses on sustainable development in the North Eastern region of India which includes the "...poorest and voiceless ethnic communities living in the far-flung un-reach villages..."(Nedan Foundation n.d). As they state within their description:

> Nedan's vision is to build a society marked by development, equality, peace and respect for human rights for all sections' where youth are involved in all developmental interventions –from bringing peace to overall holistic and sustainable developmental perspectives and vision (Nedan Foundation n.d.).

Though the foundation focuses on human rights and development in a specific region within India, it is also a part of the larger UNDP's Women and Wealth Project. This project, as part of the United Nations Development Programme, works with and for HIV positive women within Asian regions. Through its objectives it works toward development through small social enterprises, to reduce stigma and discrimination for women with HIV, and to increase awareness and education about HIV (Bamber 2012). As UN resident coordinator and UNDP representative in India, Patrice Couer-Bizot states:

> Beyond economic empowerment, the Women and Wealth Project in Assam provides a space for psycho-social support that helps women to collectively cope with the indignities and discrimination they face at home and in society as trafficked survivors and HIV positive women. It is an important process of collaboration between developing countries and learning among community organizations that is making a difference in the lives of vulnerable women in Assam. (Bamber 2012)

It is important to acknowledge the larger organizations that Weaving Destination is a part of to understand the underlying mission and aims of the organization itself. Through these framework we can understand that Weaving Destination is part of an overall objective to empower HIV positive women through the idea of sustainable economic development.

In understanding the origins and parent organizations of Weaving Destination we can take a micro look at the project itself to examine the specific aims of the organization. Focusing on the vulnerable indigenous women who are either HIV positive or have been the victims of human trafficking, Weaving Destination works within the Bodoland Territorial Council within the state of Assam in India. As stated within their organization description, "WD capitalizes and enhances the inherent inborn skill of Bodo women in weaving, and is committed to convert traditional weaving skills into income-earning opportunity for women and girls" (Nedan Foundation n.d.). Using these skills the women produce everything from clothing and lifestyle products including scarves, runners, and garments for various purposes that are then sold to the masses within South East Asia. As the Nedan Foundation explains, "Weaving Destination's business unit, while preserving the traditional Bodo's motifs, colours and weaving techniques, is attempting to design products to suit the local, national and international market" (Nedan Foundation n.d.). Thus, Weaving Destination is not just looking towards the use of traditional weaving, but using it in a way that is adaptive and sustainable in modern fashion. The profits from these designs and products are then put back into planning vocational training centers for vulnerable young girls in the region. By providing education for weaving skills as well as marketing and business knowledge, WD believes it provides empowerment and opportunity for the disenfranchised women as well as the future generation of girls in the community.

Weaving Destination has been made possible by the larger projects such as Nedan and UNDP, but is has also benefited through its association with former international Bangladesh-born model and renowned fashion designer, Bibi Russell. Russell has been featured in campaigns for designers such as Yves Saint Laurent, Karl Lagerfeld and in fashion magazines such as Vogue. Additionally, Russell has started her own line, Bibi Productions, based out of her native Bangladesh. Russell has been instrumental through her acts as spokeswoman, community figure, and an educator in the use of traditional weaving techniques in the modern fashion system. As Russell reiterates, "Women need support to develop skills that will help them to be economically independent and socially confident. What they need is self-esteem, human dignity, and empowerment for better livelihoods and sustainable income. This is what I am committed to" (United Nations Development Programme 2012). Through her association, Weaving Destination receives the recognition needed to become an even more successful program and bring its message to the international stage.

In looking at the goals and aims of Weaving Destination as well as those of the parent organizations that have enabled this program to exist, we can also consider the project within the idea of social justice. In the capabilities approach presented within the work by theorist John Alexander, ideas of equality and social justice are introduced in tandem with each other. The capabilities approach asserts the position "...in creating the greatest possible condition for the realization of basic capabilities for all" (Alexander 2008:1). In this sense, this theory sees justice in the sense of equal opportunities for all through a leveling of capabilities or opportunities. Alexander continues in detailing the expression of the capabilities approach within modern institutions. As he explains,

> ...[T]he focus of the capability approach as a theory of justice is not to level down or even out people's differences in talents, capacities and potentialities, but to design society's economic and political institutions in such a way that adequate material and social resources are available to everyone in order to possess and exercise a set of basic capabilities that go to make up a decent life. (Alexander 2008: 2)

He then continues,

> These institutional expressions of social responsibility and solidarity can be justified only to the extent that they are meant not to replace or undermine agency and personal responsibility but to facilitate them. (Alexander 2008: 2)

Through Alexander's ideas, the capabilities approach within social justice allows for development and assistance that is sustainable within communities.

Individuals would be provided opportunities that would allow for growth and subsidize for areas of inequality. In this way Weaving Destination acts within the ideas of the capabilities approach. Instead of just provide, for instance, funds for the Bodo women, UNDP and the Nedan Foundation have allowed for Weaving Destination to build the skills and knowledge so that funds can be sustainable and empowering for the women. They capitalize on the ideas of social responsibility that create agency and personal responsibility that Alexander spoke of. Fashion provides the medium in which this may be enacted through ideas of tradition and creativity expressed through the products produced. Thus, the skills taught through the project become manifested through the scarves and lifestyle products that are worn on bodies and seen in homes internationally.

Weaving Destination allows for a useful model of the connection of fashion and social justice as expressed through the capabilities approach. Through teaching modern skills to disenfranchised women in rural areas, fashion allows for empowerment and positive international connections. This empowerment is seen through monetary support and also through the development of skill and basic opportunity not provided for before as HIV positive or a victim of sex trafficking. Yet this organization does raise questions as to the reproductive quality of this model. For instance, Weaving Destination was fortunate to have the NGO financial and organizational support through the UNDP and the Nedan Foundation. Also, the connection to the recognized figure of model and designer Bibi Russell has brought additional press to the project. While positive, other endeavors might not be as fortunate to have these support systems. Regardless, it is important to recognize the possibilities present in bringing together traditional, local creativity with the global entrepreneurial mind and the effect it has upon fashion's place in social justice.

SUPPLY
CHANGE

Maureen Brewster

# Sourcing Social Justice: Fashion Designers Without Borders

In an industry that has thus far been consumed primarily by the capitalist desire to produce the maximum amount of goods at the lowest personal cost, the collateral damage has been the peoples of under-developed countries, who are often prevented from autonomous engagement or advancement within the fashion system. Fashion Designers Without Borders (FDWB) seeks to rectify this injustice, while simultaneously providing industry insiders with the tools to assist them and use their experience to influence their future design sourcing collaborations– and inspire others to do the same.

With greater consumer pressure to embrace more ethical and sustainable practices, the fashion industry has made halting progress in shifting its approach to globalized design, and has become progressively involved with bringing more geographically and socio-economically remote producers into the fashion system. This has resulted in a steady growth in organizations dedicated to facilitating such interaction, such as the Supply Change. Conceived after founder Chrissie Lam took a sabbatical from her corporate design job, the Supply Change is a means of connecting companies with artisan enterprises in a partnership to their "mutual benefit" (The Supply Change 2012). Brands like Chico's and Whole Foods are able to collaborate with endeavors such as the Andean Collection, a social development initiative based in Brooklyn that sources handmade jewelry from artisans in Ecuador (The Supply Change 2012).

Having created a means of connecting corporations with these social enterprises, Lam recognized the potential benefit of taking a more direct approach. Lam's own experiences as a designer and traveler informed her newest operation: Fashion Designers Without Borders (FDWB), which takes interested designers on specially tailored sourcing trips to engage firsthand with their potential artisan collaborators. Lam had personally engaged in these types of alliances before, on retail sourcing trips to often underdeveloped countries. "We want to create ambassadors– ambassadors that can influence change within their companies and raise awareness and action through real stories and word-of-mouth experiences," Lam says (Trend Tablet 2012).

To bring these ambassadors to these social initiatives, FDWB is itself a partnership, between the Supply Change and luxury safari company called Extraordinary Journeys. Together the two businesses have created "sourcing safaris" to Kenya, Guatemala, and Ecuador beginning in February 2013. Designers will be able to follow specially planned itineraries, with all travel and accommodations arranged in advance. The trip is tailored to be a comprehensive, efficient and inspirational guide to the region of choice, with the goal of interested designers returning not only with plans for a collaboration, but also with the desire to share their experience and contribute to the expansion and promotion of this design practice.

This business model thus seemingly aims to address two key injustices in the fashion system: access and agency by those in geographically and economically remote marketplaces, and the relative lack of global social awareness in the design industry, which often leads to unethical, unsustainable, and exploitative production practices. In merging these two issues, FDWB aims to change the framework of the fashion system from without and within; by orchestrating the introduction of corporate designers to their second and third-world counterparts, they seek to improve the access and agency of both groups to a more socially just version of design. They are engaging in the construction of a new system of fashion based on empowerment and sustainability somewhat in resonance with design scholar Earl Tai's idea of a "philosophy of distributive justice in design" which according to Tai is "not merely as an optional nicety, but as an ethical imperative" (Tai 2009: 454).

Such commitment to forging links between disparate design communities is driven from Lam's professed desire to "propel social change," and may in a limited sense exemplify the liberation sociology's goal to "[support] the action of human beings in their own liberation" (Feagin & Vera 2001: 3). Lam's effort to improve the lives of the second and third-world artisans through corporate partnership is consistent with many other design-based initiatives, such as the aforementioned Andean Collection, that seek to utilize skilled labor to create a more profitable, self-sufficient and empowered community. Perhaps design may in this sense act as a proponent of Feagin and Vera's idea of liberation sociology as a tool to "help those who are powerless become more powerful" (Feagin & Vera 2001: 35). What is different about FDWB's approach is the concept that the designers embarking on these sourcing safaris will become empowered as well, and return with the knowledge and desire to rework the system of fashion production from within. In developing this "mutually beneficial and profitable relationship" (FDWB 2012) both artisans and visiting designer alike will receive the tools they need to gain a greater amount of agency to change the character of their design communities.

Though FDWB is undoubtedly idealistic in these efforts, it is impossible to ignore the problematic nature of its business model. Ostensibly set up to benefit the un- and underemployed in economically disadvantaged regions, the company seems instead to be trading upon the exoticism of these foreign locales: from the term "sourcing safaris" to the locations chosen, there is an 'othering' taking place that detracts from the noble goal of its mission statement. The implication that these small artisan communities require the assistance of corporate partnership to bring about their own social change is troubling, to say the least. This, when taken in tandem with the strong emphasis on making the relationship into a beneficial business strategy to the visiting designers, shifts FDWB away from representing a purely moral imperative, reducing it to a facile approach towards a real problem in the design world. It also invites criticism of the very name of the company: Fashion Designers Without Borders is an explicit reference to Doctors Without Borders, the organization that brings medical treatment and "independent, impartial assistance to those most in need" (Doctors Without Borders 2012). The fact that FDWB adopts the name but does not hold itself to the same high degree of humanitarian ethics undermines the gravity of the mission of Doctors Without Borders, and begins to trivialize itself by comparison.

From one perspective we could draw parallels between FDWB and the ideals of liberation sociology as they may both aim "to translate personal troubles into public issues, and public issues into the terms of their human meaning for a variety of individuals" (Feagin & Vera 2001: 35). However, it has yet to reconcile key issues with its structure and mission– including its very name– to make it an unquestionably ethical and sustainable organization. The company has taken the first steps to create a means to enable artisans to create their own empowerment, and designers to create change in the fashion system. With further revision of its approach to integrating disparate design communities, Fashion Designers Without Borders may yet become a way to turn design sourcing into a social resource.

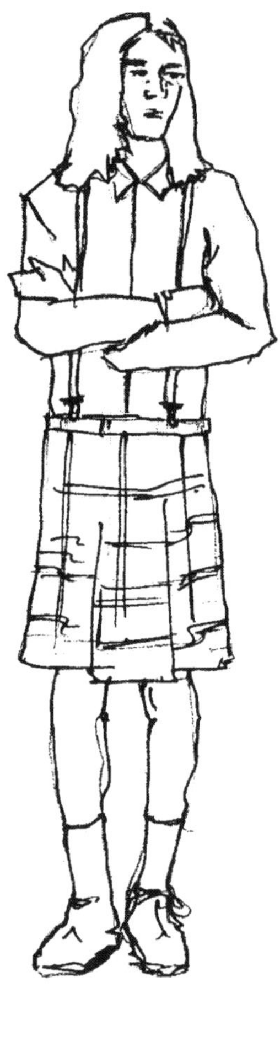

Susana Aguirre

# Meet your Maker through IOU

The IOU Project is a web portal and business that aims to curtail the prevailing disconnect between garment producers and consumers with the aim of building a clothing brand more transparent and socially responsible. Specifically, IOU works with weavers from India and craftsmen to create clothing and accessories (scarves, shoes, bags, etc.) out of handmade madras, a lightweight cotton fabric typically with plaid design, and other fabrics.

The website has a three-minute video that introduces visitors to the project's concept, explaining that IOU's story begins, "Around 1920 with an act of peaceful defiance by one of the world's greatest men who assembled one of the world's largest armies… and what they did was weave! Their revolution helped free India" (IOU - Introduction). By connecting the business' history with that of "Mahatma Gandhi and his weavers," IOU aims to impart the idea that the brand is continuing the work of liberating weavers from the oppressive conditions in which they have been living. The video states that over 20 million families depend on handloom weaving for subsistence. Furthermore, it states that this army of weavers are up against "an old enemy," the machine, which, unlike the weavers, uses a lot of energy; pollutes; fosters unemployment and makes replicas of the exact same garment.

IOU places these negative aspects of the machine against our seemingly universal desire to express uniqueness through our clothing, taking care of our environment, and the desire to "craft a better world." This cannot be reached if machines replace the work of artisans. With the statement, "we can change the way clothing is made and sold," IOU has nicely set up a scenario in which their business model is seen as a solution. The video makes it clear that this clothing brand will do things differently: instead of working with machines, IOU works with artisans; instead of mass production, IOU finds "great European craftsmen to assemble each piece;" instead of using impersonal forms of distribution, they make sure "you [the customer] know the whole story."

The video is a visual rendering of how the IOU Project differs from the unjust and environmentally unfriendly clothing businesses that persist in the fashion industry. IOU places itself on the right side of the moral compass by imparting on consumers that this brand addresses an injustice and that by becoming "part of the story," i.e. purchasing IOU products, this injustice is remedied.

One of the sections of the website that aims to show potential customers how the company works is IOU People, where you can see the life story behind the various individuals who make the clothes and the brand possible. You can search by 'role,' where artisans, weavers, trunk show hosts, and IOU people (company employees) are highlighted with a photograph and a short description. Visitors can also search by specific designs, allowing the visitor to learn about each 'item's journey' (i.e. who weaved the item, what fabric was used, and who assembled it).

The idea of traceable and transparent fashion, i.e. ethical fashion, is largely being used by companies as a marketing tool to attract customers since it responds to a growing demand to know where products come from and how they are made. In terms of traceability, IOU goes to great lengths to explain the process behind the pieces they sell. In terms of transparency, IOU offers details into the working relationship between the company and weavers. Visitors are able to know the name of the weaving cooperative he/she works for and what year he/she became a member of the cooperative.

Navigating through the various layers of information that IOU provides can be dizzying, but it speaks of the company's desire to answer all the possible questions a customer may have about the product. On the one hand, this level of knowledge provides a vehicle by which the (potential) customer is able to connect with the clothes beyond their aesthetic value, allowing for the feeling of creating personal (albeit virtual) relationships with the IOU family. However, one can question how necessary or valuable the information they provide can prove to be. What is the value behind a 15 second video of the weaver standing and smiling in front of the camera? Perhaps in their quest to build a bridge between consumer and producer, IOU can provide information that can more sincerely let customers know about the people behind the garments.

Another way in which IOU wishes for customers to feel part of the family is by allowing customers to share their own stories and 'love' for IOU products under the role of 'trunk show hosts,' in which they become curators for the site through mini e-shops within the IOU site. This business model works for IOU under the slogan of being an activity that is for "fun, profit and social good."

In writing about the branch of social sciences known as "liberation sociology", social researchers Joe Feagin and Hernan Vera stress that those who take up such a concept in their way of seeing the world, "often takes sides with, and takes the outlook of, the oppressed and envisions an end to that oppression" (Feagin & Vera 2001: 1). They further argue that the idea behind this perspective is "not just to research the social world but to change it in the direction of expanded human rights." In this sense, liberation sociology can be considered a counter-system approach, and its principles used to explain different approaches to perceive and address social injustice. The goal is to envision and create "a society where people have empathetic compassion for human suffering and a commitment to reducing that suffering" (1).

A counter-system project aims to raise "people's consciousness of the oppressive structures of the society in which we live in" (11). The IOU Project can be considered a counter-system initiative in that it aims to connect people from around the world, through clothes, with the realities of garment workers and inform them of the positive impact working with an ethical fashion business can have on these workers lives. Feagin and Vera give the example of the critical media endeavour called Project Censored which aims to "identify the underreported or ignored news stories" as this kind of counter-system approach (5). In a similar vein, IOU Project has the objective of bringing to light the stories of weavers and garment workers whose stories are rarely acknowledged or related to customers who purchase the fruits of their labor. Furthermore, IOU has as its main mission to "support the action of human beings in their own liberation."

Feagin and Vera advances that social oppression is a "systematic institutional processes which prevent some people from learning and using satisfying and expansive skills in socially recognized settings or institutionalized social processes which inhibit people's ability to... communicate with others or to express their feelings and perspective on social life in contexts where others can listen" (14). In this sense, the global fashion system is an institution that has historically silenced the histories and stories of people who work in the assembly lines of the industry. Any act that "encourages us to think critically about the socially patterned nature of the world around us" is one that can (hopefully) break the reproductions of oppression. In this way, the IOU Project aims to be a business model that first and foremost takes into consideration the positive social impact it can have on communities such as the weavers and craftsmen they work with. The way in which IOU has decided to accomplish this goal is by connecting consumers and producers through the lifecycle of garments, attempting to connect "everyday life and its constraints" as lived by garment workers. IOU is one of many a growing number of retailers that aim to expose in various ways the people behind the making of clothes. How effective IOU's approach should be analyzed further. Without these various attempts, however, we run the risk of ignoring the humanity of those who make the fashion industry possible, being further blinded to the fact that injustices are committed at every level of the industry, day in and day out.

# BODY

# MATTERS

Cally Carbone

# Downs Designs: Clothing Needs for Down Syndrome

> Dress is the way in which individuals learn to live in their bodies and feel at home in them. Wearing the right clothes and looking our best, we feel at ease with our bodies…dress is both an intimate experience of the body and a public presentation of it. (Entwistle 2000: 7)

Clothing and the body have a direct physical relationship when worn, but as established by fashion theorist Joanne Entwistle also create a social relationship for the wearer. Through these relationships, this case study seeks to speak to the practices of a company creating clothing for people with Down syndrome and its establishment of social justice through the ethics of care, based in relational factors.

Founded by Karen Bowersox in 2010, Downs Designs creates clothing for individuals with Down syndrome. Bowersox started her company after witnessing her daughter's struggle to find clothing that comfortably fit her own daughter, Bowersox's granddaughter, who has Down syndrome (Siek 2011). Bowersox wrote in the original post of her company's blog, "I started this business because my granddaughter has Down syndrome and her mother struggles to find clothes that fit her appropriately. I hope that by the time Maggie cares what she wears, she will have proper fitting clothes that she gets from her grandmother's special clothing line" (Downs Design n.d.). Common generalizations create social stigmas for people with Down syndrome. "Though Down syndrome is commonly generalized by cognitive disability and facial characteristics only, there are other physical traits that Bowersox seeks to accommodate through her company's designs—low muscle tone and small stature (Seik 2011; National Down Syndrome Society 2012). These physical traits are often the reason why off-the-rack clothing does not fit children and adults with Down syndrome. Downs Designs has developed an alternative sizing system considered "Down Sizing" in order to more justly create clothing for individuals with Down syndrome.

Simply put, Bowersox tries to fill a gap in the clothing market, to fit the physical needs of children and adults with a specific condition. As the founder of Downs Designs she seeks to develop garments that will also emotionally help anyone who ultimately wears her company's clothing, as stated in an interview,

> Most people underestimate the effect that having badly fitting clothes can have on the perception – and self-esteem – of a person with Down syndrome. "'Their entire life, this is one of their biggest challenges, and people do not know that,' Bowersox said. 'They are forced to wear ill-fitting clothes that make their difference look even more pronounced. When they put on a shirt that fits, it takes away that difference'" (Seik 2011).

The clothing styles that Downs Designs creates are designed with fit and style in mind. After two years in business, the company offers jeans in various styles and sizes for women, teens, and children, ranging in price from $16.95 to $39.95. Additionally, the company designs and sells women's long-sleeved shirts, priced $18.95 to $25.95. Each jeans and shirt design takes into account the unique body shape of someone with Down syndrome, aiming to fit garments correctly at the knees and elbows, and avoid the need roll up pant legs and shirt sleeves. Men's clothing will be available this season, fall 2012. The sizing for Downs Designs' jeans and shirts is not consistent with off-the-rack clothing sizing strategies for adults, teens or children; it is in fact based solely on measurements. Jeans sizes are determined by measurement ranges for waist and hips and labeled as sizes A-F for adults and teens, and A-G for children (Downs Designs n.d.). Also, Downs Designs offers, at a small charge, to hem any pair of jeans purchased, to further ensure proper and ideal fitting. Apparent on the company website, in product descriptions, they take care to alleviate any further discomforts a wearer might encounter, particularly for jeans, "we make them in a soft, stretchy fabric with a full elastic waistband that is also soft and stretchy…Our labels are printed on the inside pocket lining so there are no tags to irritate the skin" (Downs Designs n.d.).The most developed category for Downs Designs is women's jeans. There are four available styles that take in account different body types within the form of a woman with Down syndrome. Each style allows for buyers to associate with a particular body type, measure according to the size guide, and hopefully end up wearing a pair of jeans that feels like they were created for especially with them in mind.

Bowersox's model of "Down Sizing" seeks to include a different body type in the fashion industry. People with Down syndrome are now able to find clothing that is specifically tailored to their physical needs, because of Downs Designs. One could argue it is similar to differentiation like maternity, petite and plus sizing, in that by making slight differences to design and construction of garments, a better fit for a body type is achieved. However, "Down Sizing" is still an outlier in the fashion industry sizing system, with only more than 400,000 people living with Down syndrome in the United States, clothing made especially for their body type will continue to be a niche market (National Down Syndrome Society 2012).

Through Carol Gilligan's ethics of care, while correspondingly accepting Grace Clement's interpretation, it can be seen how Bowersox with Downs Designs seeks fairness for people with Down syndrome within the fashion industry. For the purpose of this case study, the lens of feminist, gender-based theory is removed and the ethics are understood as being interrelated with the ethics of justice, not as polar opposites. With the understanding of an ethic of care being "subjects trying to discern the specific concrete and unique factors of the situation," (Capeheart & Milovanovic 2007) and addressing Downs Designs, Bowersox sought a solution based on need factors and of course attachment, as mentioned before, her granddaughter was the original inspiration for her endeavor. She determined there were specific needs for her subject category that were not the focus or assumed responsibility of the larger mainstream fashion industry, and continues to work on creating clothing that better fits their body types. Bowersox has placed importance on the human beings her company designs for and their social contextualization. Her moral judgment can be assumed as finding an inclusion for adults, teens and children with Down syndrome in the fashion industry, where size and body differences are often discriminated.

Downs Designs may not be the ultimate justice for individuals with Down syndrome and their dress needs, but it does create a foundation for fashion to embrace a group of people with condition specific physical bodies. And even though the company has yet to design items in every imaginable product category, the dream is there. "I can't accomplish this fast enough. I want a complete line in my lifetime. I want suits. I want prom dresses," Bowersox said. "They just want to look like every other kid." (Siek 2011) Bowersox has developed products through Downs Designs that give better fitting clothing options to adults, teens and children with Down syndrome, instead of relying on off-the-rack clothing that may be uncomfortable and ill fitting; thus, minimizing perceived fashion injustices and as a result, making them socially comfortable in their own bodies.

Laura Jane Kenny

# Dressing Justly: Sit Up for Your Rights

Fashion is not known for being inclusive. Yet, the industry that is constantly knocked for only being available for the tall, the thin and the young has in recent years seen some initiatives of wider inclusion. New outlets for the fashion outsider--the short, the round and the old--can be seen in structured media like magazines and designer labels or independent forums like blogs and zines. While these types of bodies that have been previously excluded, devalued or even mocked, are now sometimes even donning the pages of major fashion magazines, not all body types are in the collective conscious of the fashion society. The body that is often left out of the fashion lexicon is that of the differently-abled person, particularly that of the person who uses a wheelchair. Although issues of access are often associated with money, inaccessibility can go beyond the pocketbook. Clothing that is not designed for a seated person is inaccessible to this demographic. Store layouts and the design of shopping centers in general may hinder the seated customer from even trying these garments on.

The person who uses a wheelchair is no stranger to being "othered" in society or in media. An article by Spencer E. Cahill and Robin Eggleston entitled, "Reconsidering the Stigma of Physical Disability: Wheelchair Use and Public Kindness," touches on the hardship of dressing the disabled body by recounting the story of a seated person while shopping in a department store:

> It was a young kid ... in the men's department. He saw me coming. He starts vigorously folding shirts that didn't need folding just so he wouldn't have to wait on me. He took a shirt, and he burst it, and he'd fold it up again.... So I just sort of stayed in the area, but after a while it was obvious that he didn't want to approach me (Cahill 1995).

Shopping, trying on clothing and having help offered when it is not desired are large themes of the struggles encountered in the the previously mentioned article. While much of this could be accredited to the lack of physically capabilities of those in wheelchairs trying on garments, there are other factors at play. These factors include the sales people training to work with those who are in wheelchairs and how the clothes are crafted. That is, much of clothing is made for those who are abled body and can dress themselves. It seems that the needs of the otherly-abled population are not met by the general fashion industry, particularly in the shopping experience.

However, this has changed in recent years as new clothing made specially for those using wheelchairs has been created. One such company is Izzy Camilleri Adaptive Clothing. Izzy Camilleri, a Canadian fashion designer, was asked to design a custom garment for a journalist who was quadriplegic. The experience and the relationship influenced Camilleri to start a line of clothing specially for those who use wheelchairs. This was one of the first lines created for "seated" clientele. This line, IZ Adaptive, sells a similar array of clothing that can be found on most online stores. However, the online portal displays the clothing on models who are sitting, giving those in wheelchairs the ability to see how the clothing would look when they wear it. IZ Adaptive offers clothing for professional, formal and casual use. IZ Adaptive keeps in mind the needs of the seated placements, focusing on crucial elements such as strategic zipper placement in order to accommodate specific needs.

Another website and fashion line, Ag Apparel, offers similar clothing. Named after the element for silver on the periodic table, Ag Apparel was created by Jordan Silver whose motto is "Let Fashion set you free and the rest will follow (Agapparel.com)." Ag Apparel focuses on making their clothes easy to wear and offers custom tailoring. Silver created Ag Apparel after her aunt passed away from Amyotrophic lateral sclerosis. Silver witnessed her aunt's struggle with her clothing and wanted to add to the solution that would allow people like her aunt to enjoy clothing and still offer them independence and dignity.

Ag Apparel and IZ Adaptive are just a few clothing companies that seek to serve seated clientele. These companies and other like them seek to serve a population that has been overlooked by the fashion industry. Although these models do not solve every problem, they do extend the chic fashion olive branch to those who are all too often--if not always--forgotten about or ignored in the fashion community. While fashion is often deemed something accessible to all--especially fast fashion and it's availability and price point, models like this shed light on former ideas and accessibility and widen it. Yet, ideas about accessibility cannot end with the creation of garments for those in wheelchairs.

Sociologists Joe Feagin and Hernan Vera suggest that people are oppressed through the social construct of our everyday and expressed in human interactions with one another on a personal and systemic level. While clothing might seem like a minute detail to some, it can be received as the furthering of an oppressive society. If society is not making clothes for these people by not designing clothes that seated customers can wear or buy themselves, these individual are outside of the general society that we consider worthy to dress. Once the fashion community has seen where we have been blind before, it should shift how we think about all the products that we sell. Perhaps this can be a new way to view the models for websites that aren't directed to the "seated" clientele but offer views for seated clientele in order to include them. Perhaps this should remind fashion publications about important factors like word choice and those that they feature. This may even shift the way that companies build their stores--allowing those who are in wheelchairs to access them.

Accessibility is laced with ideas of social justice. The idea that all things should be accessible to all people stems from concepts addressed by Loretta Capeheart and Dragan Milovanovic in their book *Social Justice: Theories, Issues and Movements*. They would suggest that social justice allows us to find the greater good for all of the possible voices, not just the loudest. If we approach this idea about accessibility with the perspective of Capeheart and Milovanovic, perhaps we can understand accessibility to be a necessary component of justice. Ideas about movement and a seated shopper remind us that our ideas of what it means for something to be accessible is not solely limited to monetary concepts. While monetary access is important to consider, lines like Ag Apparel and IZ Clothing remind us that access and lack of access come in different forms. Companies like these are excellent examples of how one group of people or even just one person can make a difference and make something like fashion more inclusive. Yet, they also stand for reminders and can create an opportunity for us to reevaluate patterns and practices that we live in based on what we have recently discovered.

I BEAT
OBESITY

Kelsey Allyn Glein

# Wellness on the Runway: the CFDA Health Initiative

Models are an integral part of the fashion system, with their influence on beauty and body image being felt far outside of the fashion industry. Models act as the face of fashion to those outside of the industry, are seen as idealized versions of the human form, and are often looked up to as role models. Just as trends in fashion change, so do trends in models. In the 1990s, "Heroin Chic" was popularized and was characterized by models with pale skin, dark circles underneath their eyes, angular bone structure, and extremely thin frames. This version of beauty was reflective of drug addiction and the heroin use that was rampant at the time. These emaciated figures, such as model Kate Moss, were largely a reaction against "healthy" models, such as Cindy Crawford. Though the "Heroin Chic" trend in models was declared to have ended with the return of "sexy" models in the 2000s, such as model Gisele Bündchen, the lingering influence of the 1990s "Heroin Chic" look remains. Though the "Heroin Chic" trend is not the only source of blame, today we still see emaciated models walk the runway, some who are underage and have eating disorders. This is a problem that the fashion industry is knowledgeable of but has largely chosen to ignore because of the desire to hire skinny women, despite the impact the ultra thin trend has both on the models and those who emulate them. Models have often been expected to adhere to dangerous ideals in order to succeed in the industry.

The healthy well-being of models is often overlooked by those both inside and outside of the fashion industry. The Council of Fashion Designers of America (CFDA) recognized this, and in January 2007 formed a health initiative "to address what has become a global fashion issue: the overwhelming concern about whether some models are unhealthily thin, and whether or not to impose restrictions in such cases" (CFDA 2012). The CFDA Health Initiative seeks to address the obvious wrong of models, as a result of working in the fashion industry, developing eating disorders and being exploited due to their underage. Eating disorders are a serious and regrettably common issue that can potentially result in death, and this initiative attempts to prevent this injustice from occurring. The CFDA believes that designers share a responsibility to protect women, young girls in particular, within the business by advocating and sending the message that beauty is health. The CFDA uses the Health Initiative as a campaign to bring awareness and to create an atmosphere that supports the well-being of these young women (CFDA 2012). The CFDA, working with the fashion industry, medical experts, nutritionists, and fitness trainers, proposed the following practical steps designed to promote wellness and a healthier working environment for models:

> Educate the industry to identify the early warning signs in an individual at risk of developing an eating disorder; Models who are identified as having an eating disorder should be required to seek professional help, and models who are receiving professional help for an eating disorder should not continue modeling without that professional's approval; Develop workshops for the industry (including designers, agents, editors, and models and their families) on the nature of eating disorders, how they arise, how we identify and treat them, and complications that may arise if left untreated; Support the well-being of younger individuals by not hiring models under the age of sixteen for runway shows; not allowing models under the age of eighteen to work past midnight at fittings or shoots; and providing regular breaks and rest - Consult the applicable labor laws found at www.labor.state.ny.us when working with models under sixteen; Supply healthy meals, snacks, and water backstage and at shoots and provide nutrition and fitness education (CFDA 2012).

The CFDA asserts that the Health Initiative is about awareness and education, not about policing, and states that it is "committed to the notion of a healthy mind and a healthy body" as there cannot be one without the other (CFDA 2012).

In dealing with this problematic issue, supporting health while at the same time satisfying the image industry, the CFDA Health Initiative has been successful in that it has brought awareness of issues with model health into public discourse. Previously, the fashion world had not overtly or publicly addressed or even acknowledged many of these issues dealing with extreme thinness or underage workers in the modeling industry (Wintour 2012). Though the model is given a place of prestige in our culture, not all achieve success on the level of models like Kate Moss, Gisele Bündchen, and Naomi Campbell. Many models are adored and well-paid, but not all are given this same luxury. However, despite the admiration that models receive, they are often thought of as beautiful dehumanized images, not workers who deserve the same right and protection as anyone else (Ziff 2012). Models are constantly under the gaze of others, and must remain under surveillance in order to succeed. Acknowledging this oversight and agreeing that models are often overworked, underfed, and underage, many designers and publications have stepped up to support the CFDA in their efforts, including Vogue. The Health Initiative has encouraged editors, designers, photographers, and casting directors alike to "share the responsibility of fostering a climate where a vital and healthy physique is lauded and encouraged" within the fashion industry (Wintour 2012). Vogue has committed to depicting healthy body images in their magazine and to not knowingly work with models under the age of sixteen or models that appear to have an eating disorder (Critchell 2012). Though these are small steps, they are certainly important in the fight for labor and health standards in the modeling industry. The fashion industry is just a piece of the puzzle in the fight against eating disorders, as there are larger societal issues that act as creators of these issues. Anna Wintour, Editor-in-Chief of Vogue, encourages us not to oversimplify these crucial issues, however, and purports that:

> Fashion has often been (wrongly) held up as an active agent in making women want to be excruciatingly thin, ignoring the complex genetic and psychosocial factors that contribute to eating disorders. Knee-jerk condemnation of many of the girls working today who are naturally blessed with slim bodies and exercise and eat well to maintain them is to be scrupulously avoided. So, too, is ignoring the way that obesity levels are rocketing upward, especially among the young, paving the way for all sorts of problems in the future. Making a stand with the Health Initiative signals renewed efforts to make our ideal of beauty a healthy one (Wintour 2012).

While the fashion industry is only one of many contributors to unhealthy body image that leads to eating disorders, it may be notable that they have recognized this injustice that they are a part of and are attempting to correct it.

However important the CFDA Health Initiative is in making the public and fashion industry aware of model health issues, it does not do enough to reduce the injustices. Sara Ziff, founder of The Model Alliance, applauds Vogue for its pledge to improve the working conditions of models and persuading the industry to take better care of its young, and asserts that the move is an important one for the fashion world (Critchell 2012). Vogue, according to Ziff, has a penchant for hiring models who are minors, so for them to commit to not longer using models under the age of sixteen marks an evolution in the fashion industry (Critchell 2012). Yet Ziff states there is still much to be done for models in the fashion industry, and she has set out with The Model Alliance to implement legal protections for models, specifically those who are underage. Ziff believes that a crackdown on model age is just as important as a crackdown on model weight, as the use of underage models is linked to financial exploitation, eating disorders, interrupted schooling, and an overall lack of empowerment for models in the workplace (Critchell 2012).

Recently, Ziff testified before the New York State Department of Labor advocating for regulations for models that are minors. Though Ziff appreciates the efforts the CFDA has made with the Health Initiative, she adamantly states that "the industry has tried self-regulation. It hasn't worked. The Council of Fashion Designers of America has made efforts through its Health Initiative to promote the message that 'beauty is health.' But their guidelines are more lax than New York labor laws, and they are not an enforcement body" (2012). For the injustice against models to be truly reduced, laws must be amended and enforced. While the CFDA Health Initiative has done an adequate job of outlining what the ideal guidelines for modeling in the fashion industry should be, they have not and cannot make sure that these guidelines are followed. Ziff asserts that models need to have a voice in the workplace in order for their basic working conditions to be improved and for eating disorders to stop being encouraged (2012). Ultimately, Ziff says that "while the CFDA's recognition of eating disorders among models is a huge step forward, their guidelines designed to promote wellness are just the beginning" (2012).

The media and the CFDA itself have recognized the success of the CFDA Health Initiative much as Ziff has: as raising consciousness but not solving the problem of injustice against models. Eric Wilson states that in the past five years, there has been "measurable improvement in the prevailing ideal of beauty as seen on the runways" and says that many of the top working models today reflect a changing aesthetic toward healthier figures and at least some representation of diversity in race and age (2012). He goes on to say, however, that still season after season, we see models that are dangerously thin or as young as fourteen (Wilson 2012). The CFDA recognizes that there is still much work to be done. When asked to assess the Health Initiative, both Diane von Furstenberg (President of the CFDA) and Steven Kolb (Chief Executive of the CFDA) noted that it has been successful in creating public awareness and dictating to the fashion industry that eating disorders cannot be the model standard, but that many strides forward were still required to really solve these deep-set issues (Wilson 2012). The National Eating Disorders Association has thanked the CFDA for assisting in educating the fashion industry and the public on eating disorders and for beginning to check models' identification to verify their age, providing hope that change can happen in the industry.

Economist Amartya Sen presents us with the theory of effective power, which states that "if someone has the power to make a change that he or she can see will reduce injustice in the world, then there is a strong social argument for doing just that" (Sen 2008: 335). This obligation of effective power in fighting injustice that Sen purports can be applied to the responsibility that the fashion industry must take for models. Clearly, the fashion industry has now recognized the problem and injustice of models being underweight and underage, and it can be argued that they have a social responsibility to right this wrong. This, responsibility, according to Ziff, goes further than the education and awareness that the CFDA Health Initiative has enacted (2012). The fashion industry has the ability to make a huge difference in the lives of models, and Sen might suggest that they not only have a responsibility to enact justice for models, but an obligation (Sen 2008: 336). Moving from idea to action on these issues of model health would make the world less unjust than it currently is. The fashion industry has long been resistant to change in this area, but with the CFDA Health Initiative and now the Model Alliance, seems to be moving in a more just direction to protecting models. Ultimately, while the CFDA Health Initiative has reduced the injustices on model health that it has set out to fight, there is still a long way for the fashion industry to go in order to be truly successful in righting this wrong.

THE MODEL ALLIANCE

RALPH LAUREN

Maureen Brewster

# Ralph Lauren Glamorizes the Plus-Sized Body

The Ralph Lauren label considers itself an innovator in the branding of lifestyle (Ralph Lauren Media LLC 2012), and is adept at using advertising campaigns that communicate that lifestyle by telling a story. It's difficult to say what sort of story that they were attempting to tell in a particularly notorious image from their Blue Label's fall 2010 campaign, in which size four model Filippa Hamilton was Photoshopped to near emaciation, but it was definitely not the wholesome, sporting image of American casual luxury with which they have come to be associated. Though Ralph Lauren quickly retracted the photo, it drew media attention for epitomizing the lengths to which the fashion industry will go to depict an increasingly untenable body ideal.

The idea that the fashion industry should promote a more honest representation of the body is hardly new, but with a society that is increasingly weight-sensitive and highly critical of the industry's standards and practices, there is a growing call for reform that is slowly being answered by the fashion media community. *Vogue* announced earlier this year that it would no longer feature underage or visibly underweight models in its pages, and *Seventeen* has made a vow that it will no longer aggressively retouch young models' images. Within the world of couture and major labels, however, scant progress has been made in incorporating a more diverse standard of physical proportions. Now, the very same company whose over-enthusiastic Photoshopping contributed to this rising sentiment for reform has announced a change of its own: Ralph Lauren has hired plus-sized model Robyn Lawley, whose 6 foot 2 inch, size 12-frame is a radical departure from the skeletal figure that Hamilton's body was whittled down to. Ralph Lauren is the first major label to hire a plus-sized model, and it is yet to be seen how other companies will follow, or indeed if they will at all. Plus-sized models have traditionally been relegated to less prominent positions in the industry, making this decision significant as an important first step in correcting a longstanding injustice: the invisibility of larger bodies in fashion advertising.

According to Aristotle (384-382 B.C.) justice is teleological: in order to determine whether a practice is just, we must first determine its *telos*, or purpose towards a final cause. Secondarily, as justice is honorific, we must reason about the virtues that are being honored in order to argue the purpose, or telos, of a practice (Sandel 2009: 186). In short, an Aristotelian examination of the relative social justice of Ralph Lauren's hiring of Robyn Lawley must include a discussion about the purpose of hiring a plus-sized model, and what principles the company's decision is honoring.

Ralph Lauren's emphasis on refined sportswear defines its advertising campaigns; if models are not actually shown participating in sport, they are often photographed participating in a sport or at a sporting event, or even simply in an outdoor setting; this reinforces the brand's idealization of sport. The telos of the brand, then, is to produce clothing that reflects this idealized image through its goods, and the telos of the advertising is to package this idealized image as a commodity form.

A fashion label's selection of models is part of complex system of branding and advertising, which underlines the primary telos of models: to sell. Models are typically selected to represent a company due to a set of physical characteristics that embody that company's projected image of style, in order to attract consumers and sell them that company's goods.

In this context, the telos of hiring of Lawley would be to reinforce Ralph Lauren's branded image in two ways. First, Lawley's presence is a means by which Ralph Lauren can distance itself from their aforementioned gaffe of so drastically manipulating the image of Filippa Hamilton, which seriously undermined their image. Secondly, though Robyn Lawley is considered plus-sized in the fashion world due to her dress size, she has an athletic figure, which is certainly curvier than the typical fashion model but can hardly be considered fat. This makes her an ideal medium between the highly stylized image of the body of the svelte modelesque body, and that of the average plus-sized body, a figure that will resonate positively with image-conscious consumers of all sizes. Kathleen LeBesco argues that this is a "media strategy adopted in order to present fat in an anti-political way;" showing women whose bodies do not stray beyond culturally accepted attractiveness– not "as political, just prettier than anyone had realized"– allows the media to avoid appearing overly accepting of fat bodies, which would draw overt criticism to practices of the fashion industry and those that fund it (2004: 71). Lawley's attractive, size 12 frame is a safe way of negating the company's prior missteps, allowing them to display themselves as progressive without sacrificing their position within the fashion industry.

With that telos, or purpose, in mind, we move the discussion of justice as honorific. What virtues is Ralph Lauren rewarding in its selection of Robyn Lawley to represent the brand? At first glance, Ralph Lauren is honoring Lawley's physical attractiveness as well as her larger size; by doing so, they are ostensibly honoring the virtue of diversity and inclusion by increasing the representation of previously marginalized body types in fashion. However, an important indicator of the virtues the company was honoring is the terms under which Lawley was hired: Isabel Wilkinson specifically states in her September 19, 2012 article for the Daily Beast that her image will be used solely "for in-store advertising and PR purposes," but not for more public campaigns. This means that while you may encounter Lawley's figure in Ralph Lauren stores, it is doubtful that she will be included in print or public advertising. What could at first be seen as a move to represent a greater variety of body types thus becomes a less cohesive gesture that seems to indicate an underlying ambivalence; a "non-political" gesture, as LeBesco would say, that "connotes acceptance" without directly challenging unacceptable standards (2004: 71). It therefore looks as if Ralph Lauren is honoring appearance more than anything, and that the presence of a plus-sized model is not so much a show of shifting body image ideals as it is simply that: a show.

Regardless, Ralph Lauren's inclusion of a body type that differs from the typical unattainable standards of thinness set by the fashion industry is nonetheless a step towards developing a more accepting and just society. The field of social justice, as social researchers Joe Feagin and Hernan Vera (2001) describe it, involves "totally restructuring the larger framework of social relations for the common good" (13). While Robyn Lawley's work for Ralph Lauren does not totally restructure the fashion industry's practices of visual representation, or even completely change the way in which the company itself approaches the issue, its modest approach towards justice may yet challenge the rest of the industry to change its practices and incorporate a greater variety of bodies in fashion media.

Such a change has the potential to impact the way that larger bodies are perceived by society. A recent British study suggests that the media has conditioned viewers to prefer "super slim" bodies: participants who were consistently shown images of plus-sized models were more adverse afterwards to thin models, which suggests that "increasing the diversity of body shapes and sizes portrayed in the media could rebalance our views about our own bodies in an emotionally healthy way" (NY Daily News 2012). While Ralph Lauren is far from committing to such a goal, the inclusion of Robyn Lawley in their brand is welcomed as a positive decision to portraying plus-sized models in a more just fashion.

Susana Aguirre

# Marimacho: Does the Gender Fit?

"Marimacho is classic fashion for the unconventionally masculine" the brand Marimacho's website states. The founders, Crystal González-Alé and Ivette González-Alé, make it clear that their product responds to a specific aesthetic inclination, "the modern queer aesthetic," that, as they see it, is not satisfied by the mainstream clothing market. Ranging from tops, bottoms, outerwear, swimwear, and accessories, the items designed for the Marimacho customer aim to satisfy any "masculine woman's wardrobe." Based in Brooklyn, NY, the two pillars of Marimacho are social responsibility in production (their products are produced "at a women-owned factory in New York City's Garment District") and with their product, correct an injustice that prevails in fashion.

One of the main motivations for creating Marimacho were Crystal's personal frustrations and challenges in finding clothes that fit in size and aesthetics. This is true for all men and women of different ages, sizes and unique tastes who at one point or another encounter difficulties in finding clothes that respond to their individual needs. Marimacho, then, responds to an inequality in the fashion market specific to a particular frustration that speaks of a larger issue. A hypothesis hardly considered is that the frustrations some women feel because they're unable find a certain style or size may be due to an industry-wide assumption that certain styles of dress are meant for the male body and others for the female body.

The shirt is an item that exemplifies how Marimacho is addressing the issue. Thought of as the classic men's fashion item, the shirt is primarily produced and marketed for the male body. While it's not uncommon to see a shirt in the women's section (the woman's/men's spatial and abstract separation in fashion is a connected form of discrimination) these are usually produced to appeal to a feminine aesthetic.

Feminine and masculine aesthetics are predominantly advertised and displayed as corresponding to women and men, respectively. Notions of femininity and masculinity help construct personal identities, regardless of gender. In this sense, women who identify with masculine aesthetics instead of feminine aesthetics are not represented in mainstream fashion [1]. With this prevailing, socially constructed binary, mainstream fashion hinders the construction of identities. Marimacho can be considered an example of queering fashion: transforming prevailing notions of clothes within the fashion industry to respond to a diversity of aesthetic inclinations. A 'queer act' is defined as "any act that challenges, questions, or provokes the normal, the acceptable," says Elisa Kreisinger (Kreisinger 2012).

As stated by social theorists Loretta Capeheart and Dragan Milovanovic, it is imperative to understand how dominant and non-dominant forms of justice come to be institutionalized and applied, who is excluded in these assertions, and how must these be corrected in order to justly serve all (Capeheart & Milovanovic 2007: 1). Mainstream fashion, which is usually seen as just in the sense that it is plural in its designs and prices, in reality excludes a large population when it applies the rigid male/female binary in producing and presenting clothing.

We must ask ourselves who is not represented within mainstream fashion norms and what the implications are in the construction of identities. Marimacho's Crystal identifies herself as "a masculine-identified cis woman", which indicates her aesthetic inclination is "othered" within the institutionalized or normalized fashion codes of women's apparel. This form of injustice, as it deprives people from realizing their full potential as individuals, can be corrected by actions that create accessibility and the possibility for certain underrepresented groups to express their identity (under the same circumstances) as other groups.

British philosopher and proponent of utilitarianism, John Stuart Mill (1806-1873), suggested that in relation to the utility of every person, "actions are right in proportion as they tend to promote happiness; wrong as they tend to produce the reverse of happiness" (Capeheart & Milovanovic 2007: 18). Happiness can be interpreted in many ways. In this example, happiness can be associated with the ability to achieve self-respect and self-appreciation. Design scholar Earl Tai notes that philosopher John Rawls includes self-respect within the primary goods imperative to a person's ability to function and contribute to society. From this perspective, self-respect is thus a core component of the dressed self.

In the book *Capabilities and Social Justice,* John M. Alexander explains that economist Amartya Sen sees the "opportunities that people have to nurture and to exercise their capacities" as productive humans as imperative when considering justice (Alexander 2008). These capacities are either enhanced or hampered by the familial, social and political conditions in which one lives. One could argue that equal accessibility to clothes and clothing environments that do not limit one's ability to choose a feminine or masculine aesthetic is necessary to nurture capacities. Women are indeed free and able to shop in the men's section but she is subject to stigmatization.

Alexander further notes that "justice is fulfilled when individuals have relevant basic capabilities, whether or not they are actualized into corresponding functionings" (Alexander 2008: 71). In order for individuals to have equal capabilities they should first have the equal opportunity to develop these capabilities, and a main factor in this development is having equal access to environments and objects that can enhance one's well-being. As Tai suggests, "our society cannot presume to be giving all members a fair and equal opportunity for success without considering the distribution of design value." (Tai 2009: 457)

We cannot presume that the production, spatial ordering, and advertisement of products that rigidly assumes the feminine aesthetic is solely for women and the masculine aesthetic is solely for men, allows an equal opportunity for identity formations.

Tai quotes from design journalist Virginia Postrel's essay 'A Case for Distributive Justice in Design,' where she argues that: "Human beings don't wait for aesthetics until they have full stomachs and a roof that doesn't leak. They do not pursue aesthetic needs only when basic needs have been satisfied. ... Aesthetics is not a luxury, but a universal human desire" (Tai 2009: 457). Tai's argument is that access to the tangible benefits of design and visual stimuli should not be placed on the back burner, to be considered only after the fulfillment of, what are considered, basic needs. Doing so would be to accept that these benefits are a luxury for a privileged population whose basic needs are taken cared of.

While aesthetic choice does not need to be connected to sexual identity, dress as a form of expression has been an important form of empowering queer communities. In "Skirting The Issue: Lesbian Fashion for the 1990s" Inge Blackman and Katheryn Perry dismiss a prevailing stereotype that clothing cannot be a key component in identity formation for lesbian women. To the contrary, the article states there are many "lesbians for whom style is a conscious statement of gay identity " (Blackman & Perry 1990). In addition to providing a vehicle through which one can express personal identity, clothing also provides a "visual connection" with a particular community. Furthermore, Blackman and Perry argue that, "lesbian fashion is [about] making statements".

We take for granted the bias that underlies the most common of items like the bathing suits designed and available in the women's section, which assumes that all women identify with feminine silhouettes. Marimacho put out a line this summer of swim/summer wear called 'Souvenir Collection.' They describe their 'Super Boi Swim Brief" as an item that can "rescue you from gender conforming bathing bottoms" (Marimachobk.com). In an interview with performance artist Sir Lady indee, in the Marimacho website, she says, "Queer fashion is innovation. It's all about the transcendence of norms through wearing the clothes that look good on you, the clothes that make you feel most like you."

**Notes:**

[1]. For a wonderfully recent example of this binary at play beyond fashion products, see video of Ellen Degeneres commenting on the new pens "For Her" by Bick, http://www.upworthy.com/boom-roasted-heres-why-you-dont-ask-a-feminist-to-hawk-your-sexist-product?c=ufb1

M

&CONFUSED
45
FASHION ABLE?
ALEXANDER McQUEEN
GUEST EDITOR ISSUE

Alessandro Esculapio

# Legs by McQueen: Aimee Mullins' Prosthetic Fashion

A few people in the fashion world have generated such an interesting debate as Aimee Mullins has in the last fifteen years. Since her celebrated photoshoot for a 1998 issue of the magazine Dazed and Confused, she has been questioning body ideals as well as the relationship between fashion, prostheses and disability. Through the powerful medium of fashion, she raised awareness of topics that are mostly overlooked in the public realm.

Mullins is a double-amputee paralympian athlete who also worked as a model for photographer Nick Knight in 1998 and designer Alexander McQueen in 1999, and as actress for Matthew Barney's film cycle Cremaster. She also worked in the advertisement industry and has actively promoted the work of prosthetics designers such as Van Phillips, who is the creator of her famous 'Cheetah legs', with which she also appeared on the cover of Dazed and Confused bearing the provocative title 'Fashion-able?'.

The discourse fostered by Mullins is bidirectional: on the one hand, she brings prosthetics and disability in the fashion imagery, in the design sphere and in the realm of visual art, thus redefining the concept of desirable body; on the other hand, she addresses the ideas of fashionability and identity within the prosthetic discourse, one that is usually relegated to the medical field. As she said on the occasion of her speech at TED in February 2009, one of her aims is to have people "stop compartmentalizing form, function and aesthetic" and show through her work a way to redefine and merge these concepts.

When it comes to the relationship between design and disability, discretion is usually the key-word: "The priority for design for disability has traditionally been to enable, while attracting as little attention as possible" (Pullins 2009: 15). Disability tends to be represented and enacted as invisible and when it becomes visible, we often experience a feeling of discomfort and uneasiness. This is true of most body modifications with medical and aesthetic aims: the idea is that of 'correct' and 'conform' the body according to what is socially acceptable or seen as such, to what we call body ideals.

Mullins still uses prostheses, she still conforms her body to what is seen as a 'complete' and 'fully functional' body (we must not forget that she was first an athlete), but at the same time she makes her prostheses visible. As the proud owner of twelve pair of prosthetic legs, she employs them to create different images of herself (Mullins 2009). In addition to her famous 'Cheetah legs', designed to enhance her athletic performances, she also has, among others, what she calls 'Barbie legs', which make her taller, a pair of legs carved in wood, with which she modeled for McQueen in 1999, and jellyfish-like prostheses that she wore for one of her roles in Cremaster. She claims to have the power to personalize her body, to become the architect of her own identity and, at the same time, to redefine what would normally be seen as a disability by turning it into a super-ability (Mullins 2009).

Mentioning the ironic reaction of a friend who told her it was unfair that she could become taller by switching her prostheses, Mullins stated that for her "It's no longer a conversation about overcoming deficiency. It's a conversation about augmentation, it's a conversation about potential" (Mullins 2009). Her aim is that of creating a more positive image of disability, of offering an alternative perspective on it; fashion can be seen as a helpful tool in this respect: "Fashion ... might be seen as being largely concerned with creating and projecting an image: making the wearer look good to others and feel better about themselves" (Pullins 2009: 15). But does the image of Mullins help disabled people or amputees really feel good about themselves? Or does it create another standard to which they feel compelled to live up to?

Some academics like Vivian Sobchack and Steven L. Kurzman, both amputees themselves, or Marquard Smith advise against the idea of 'prosthetic' as futuristic and 'posthuman', underlining how this metaphor is a manifestation of what is knows as technofetishism: "By technofetishism, I refer simply to that well-known and widespread series of cultural practices acted out by academics, writers, artists, and others who fetishize technology in their writings and art making - both within the confines of their intellectual communities and in everyday life" (Smith in Smith and Morra 2006: 43).

As she recounts her personal experience with prostheses, Sobchack argues that it is important that we distinguish between the metaphorical and the literal. This means that we have keep in mind that everyday life with prostheses is often far less glamorous and liberating than Mullins'. She also points out that average people do not have access to so many and diverse pairs of legs, let alone legs created by designers, whose signature entails higher prices. Among the several factors that prevent average amputees from experiencing a sense of power and liberation, Sobchack also mentions other practical issues such as health insurances and maintenance costs. Mullins thus appears to be privileged in comparison.

Nevertheless, albeit skeptically, Sobchack acknowledges Mullins' position: "However ironically paradoxical and politically incorrect, for Mullins' practical purposes the prosthetic fantasies articulated here are all potentially liberating. Indeed, Aimee Mullins' 'Cheetah legs' have allowed her to set world sprinting records and her 'Barbie legs' have allowed her a successful career as a fashion model" (Sobchack 2006: 36).
Mullins is believed to foster 'prosthetic fantasies' and the idea that technology can help us overcome our universal human limits. This is a very risky position in that, while partially subverting the idea of an amputee as someone who "lacks" something, the use of prosthetics still symbolizes the willingness to conform to the normative body before even transcending it.

Smith underlines also how Mullins' image was perceived by the medias: "The tabloid newspapers, popular magazines, and serious new sources responded to these images by concentrating on Aimee Mullins as the figure of quintessential Cyborgian sex kitten rather than as an amputee" (Smith in Smith & Morra 2006: 56). She then goes on to argue that Mullins' body does not challenge "any aesthetic conventions of beauty" or "offer...potentially disruptive possibilities" as she participates in her fetishization and does "little more than pay lip service to the affirmative politics of disability identity" (Smith in Smith & Morra 2006: 59). Mullins is indeed not only a beautiful woman, but also both an athlete and a model. She is thus able to run as fast as an average runner (if not faster, thanks to her 'Cheetah legs') and to comfortably walk on the runway among professional models. Her body hardly seems to move and behave like those of average amputees, so that the participation of disabled people becomes a virtual, rather than real, one.

Such a critique, though, undermines Mullins' role in raising awareness of disability in the public realm, as well as her ability to create debate around medical design and fashion. She constitutes an example of how "medical design...needs to appreciate that fashion often moves forward through extreme and even controversial work, and to welcome this influence within design for disability" (Pullins 2009: 38).

If fashion is often concerned with creating an appealing image, the aesthetic quality of Mullins' prosthetic legs is of high relevance in her self-fashioning. By having them created by artists and designers, she claims to consider them more than simple prostheses; she rather underlines their connection to art: "Poetry matters. Poetry is what elevates the banal and neglected object to the realm of art" (Mullins 2009). This a principle generally considered in interior design for instance, but seldom in design for disability. This also brings aesthetics at the center of individual concerns in everyday life. As design scholar Earl Tai wrote, "The spiritual benefits that can be wrought by the arts are not always second to our physical needs" (Tai 2009: 457).

Mullins also does not hide the pleasure of being able to change her legs as she changes her clothes (Pullins 2009: 31-33). Just like every garment is different depending on which designer created it, her pairs of legs have to look different one from the other, they have to look fashionable. Again, she subverts the idea of medical design as necessarily discrete. By incorporating the concept of fashionability to her prosthetic legs, Mullins creates a new image of design for disability, one that goes beyond its traditional canons. She also claims that introducing the disability discourse in the fashion world, usually seen as frivolous, is coherent with her attempt to subvert general beliefs on disability (Mullins 2011).

Mullins' legs carved in wood designed by Alexander McQueen also embody the growing importance of the designer's role in this field. Eyeglasses for instance, originally considered prosthetics, are nowadays designed by almost every fashion house: "The very fact that mild visual impairment is not commonly considered to be a disability, is taken as a sign of the success of the eyeglasses" (Pullins 2009: 16). A surprising 20% of purchasers order designer eyewear with nonprescription lenses (Pullins 2009: 17), showing how eyeglasses are even seen as desirable nowadays. Could something similar happen with legwear as well? Will designers have a new collection of prostheses coming out seasonally?

# JUST FABRIC

ATION

CLEAN CLOTHES CAMPAIGN

Laura Jane Kenny

# Hung Out to Dry: The Clean Clothes Campaign

The Clean Clothes Campaign is an alliance of organizations that seek to improve working conditions through the support of the workers in the garment industry. This campaign was created in efforts to thwart the social injustices seen in the poor working conditions of labourers in the garment industry. The Clean Clothes Campaign, or the CCC, started in 1989. In efforts to improve working conditions, they aim to educate workers and consumers through lobbying companies and government. This alliance spans fifteen European countries and has members from trade unions to non-government organizations. The network is made up of more than 200 organizations and unions located in countries where garments are produced. They help the CCC to identify local problems and consequently objectives in these countries as well as cooperating with groups which focus on labour rights in the United States, Canada and Australia. The interest that they cover included women's rights, consumer advocacy and poverty reduction.

On their website, the CCC claims to focus on a number of principles. Their first principle listed highlights the importance that the CCC gives to a safe working condition. The CCC states that this right should be available to all workers "regardless of sex, age, country of origin, legal status, employment status or location (Clean Clothes Campaign)." They describe a good and safe working condition as a place where workers can exercise "their fundamental rights to associate freely and bargain collectively and earn a living wage which allows them to live in dignity."

The CCC focuses on the livelihood and the empowerment of the workers who partake in the production process. In this vein of thought, the CCC highlights the importance of the workers knowing their rights through education and training. The CCC also encourages the workers to employ leadership through organizing themselves, believing that workers can best assess their needs and rights when they are the ones asserting their rights. The CCC encourages this to be done through public campaigns or other initiatives that speak to the rights violations going on during garment production. The development of strategies to address these issues is also strongly encouraged. It can be seen in the principles laid out by the CCC that they wish for the workers themselves to be involved in this process as directly as possible.

Other principals that the CCC focuses on are centered around the consumer or those who are not part of the production process. One of these principles focuses on the public's right to know where and by what process the garments are made. While they support the public's action, they mention that they do not generally endorse or promote boycotts as an action tool. The CCC also seeks the action beyond the individual, imploring national governments and international authorities to fulfill what the CCC sees as an obligation to address issues of worker's rights. Beyond this, the CCC also addresses that the industries for which this production happens has an obligation to become involved in the quest for rights as these companies and retailers have positions of power that could be used. Some ways the CCC believes this can be done could be through transparent working conditions and through the adoption of a code of labour practice that allows for ethical working conditions. In order to maximise these efforts, the CCC believes it would be best for trade unions and NGOS to cooperate nationally, regionally and globally in order to improve condition on an international level.

The CCC and its efforts clearly seek to find safe working conditions for all people, focusing on those who are engrossed in the physical work of the garment and apparel industry, being an industry that has been rightly criticized for the poor working conditions that labours have to produce garments in. Karl Marx's writing was largely centered on labor and production and his theories can be directly applied to the desire for rights in this labor market. In his writing, Marx discussed how the form of the production shaped the relations around the people in and outside of that production. An example given in the text is that of an assembly line. If we consider this concept on a large scale, this theory can be applied to the labor that is used to create the clothes we wear. It is interesting to think that those who make these garments that we wear very visibly--that the point of these garments is to someone outwardly tell who we are through a prominent visual culture--are made in very hidden, secret places. This surely influences the relationship not only of the labors, but of the common concept of production in relation to consumption. Marx theories on class seems to fall in line with that of the CCC. Marx would suggest that the class that is being oppressed, the working class, must be the class the leads the reform or the revolution. In fact, Marx would encourage a revolutionary consciousness to arise in the working class and that this conscious requires experience in this class struggle. What constitutes justice can play out in four ways being: instrumental Marxist, structural Marxist, structural interpellationist and constitutive Marxist. Instrumental Marxist analysis suggest that those who have the economic power also have the political power. The CCC's desire for the industries to be involved with the quest for rights seems to give a nod to this way of thinking, admitting that the companies hold a certain power in the struggle. Structural Marxist which focus on the exchange of commodities warns that equal standards cannot be applied to differences because it is inherently unequal. This branch of Marxism could also be applicable to the desires of the CCC in that they recognize that money for one's labor does not make the labor just. There needs to be much more than a transaction to create an equal system. Structural interpellationist also would fall in line with the efforts of the CCC as it ask for the involvement of the governing power to create legislation that would create a more fair system.The fourth model of Marxism suggest that the search for a just society is an ongoing process as those who are seeking justice are constantly growing and learning how to seek justice based on their cultural language and situation (Capeheart 2007).

The Clean Clothing Campaign has made a substantial impact through a variety of campaigns and alliances. One of their most recent success can be seen by Versace's announcement on the banning of sandblasting. A practice that runs unacceptable health risk, sandblasting has been banned by companies including Levis-Strauss and Hennes & Mauritz (H&M). While banning the practice of sandblasting can be critiqued as it is only removing one dangerous practice from a smorgasbord of unhealthy working conditions, it is a success for the Clean Clothing Campaign nonetheless.

If we apply the logic shared by philosopher Slavoj Zizek regarding ethical consumerism, we can see a problematic aspect of the Clean Clothing Campaign. While the CCC sheds light on the many horrors involved in the garment industry, it also only solves symptoms of much larger problem. If we take the Versace ban as an example, we can see that Versace banning sandblasting does not necessarily make the production of their clothing ethical by changing one aspect of their production. However, the problem that we face, as we often do, is that these little steps are often all that we can take. Should the CCC not try to solve any problems until they can solve all them? The CCC seems to proceed the way many other nonprofit and ethically charges organizations do--they seem to be ticking away at a small aspect of a huge problem in order to do something.

It seems that the theories present in the different model of Marxist thought are used by the CCC as they seek to create a more just working environment. As we seek to understand how fashion can be socially just, I would argue that we would not overlook the importance of the production. In many areas of consumption, the process of how the items come to the consumer is minimized, unknown or ignored. In a similar way that the average consumer has little idea of how the food at their local grocer comes to the market, many clothing consumers have little idea of where their clothing comes from nor how it's made. The continual struggle to seek a just working environment needs to be done by all classes or groups of people. While unethical production has not disappeared, this campaign has made strides in addressing issues that had largely gone unnoticed. To consider this alongside other efforts, this campaign provides a tool for those who seek to make the garment industry more just, even if it is one company at a time.

SOLIDARITY

Minna Shim

# Credit for Creativity: Fine Line Production

Han, Mel, and Chong—few of the many names that remain faceless and unrecognized in the fashion industry. Names that are buried by the incessant drone of sewing machines. Names that will be forever lost in the urban landscape of the garment district. Unfortunately, not only are their names unknown, but their work as well. As members of Fine Line Production, Han, Mel, and Chong work with over 30 designers to translate sketches into tangible creations (Lee 2012). Specializing in pattern making and grading/marking, production companies like Fine Line Production can be found all over the garment district and create most of everything we see on the New York runways (better known designers have their own production teams) (Moon 2011). Draping, pattern making, grading/marking, sewing, and the plethora of other creative skills and techniques required to transform 2D ideas into 3D forms—contrary to common assumption—are not always executed by the designer.

When asked to give a rough estimate as to how much production teams contribute to the creation of the final garment, Han Lee the owner of Fine Line Production, smiles and confidently asserts that over 50% is completed by "workers" like himself (Lee 2012). Once a designer presents a sketch and describes their collection, Lee and his team get to work and figure out the rest; they design and engineer patterns and construct garments by experimenting with fabrics, cuts, and sewing techniques. Lee and his team must envision what the garment will look like coming down the runway, hanging in the stores, and when customers take it home. Lee emphasizes the important role his team plays in determining the silhouette, structure, and movement of the garment (Lee 2012). Yet sadly, the credit and praise only goes to the designer.

As Lee continues to describe his profession, he states that the relationship between his team and the designer is symbiotic: without the designers, they wouldn't have any work and without them, the designers would only have sketches. Lee eloquently states, "The designer's success is our success, and our success is the designer's success (Lee 2012)." However, this interdependence goes unnoticed and garment experts like Lee are invisible to the audience, concealed by the hype and media surrounding the creative genius of the designer. In the rare occasions Lee and his cohorts are mentioned, they are referred to as "workers," "manual laborers," or "resources to the designers." Seldom are they acknowledged for their creative abilities and capacity for originality, innovation, and artistry. In the handful of times designers offer "behind-the-scenes" footage, never is the designer shown creating the garment, it is always an unrecognizable figure sewing, draping, cutting—someone that becomes a transparent "worker", a faceless body.

Only when the designer is taken out of the picture is the production team recognized. When John Galliano was fired for his sudden controversy before the presentation of the Christian Dior Fall 2011 RTW collection, the production team took his place and received the applause—introduced as the 'seamstresses' and 'craftsmen' and all dressed in identical white lab coats (Blanks 2011).

Regardless of the creativity required to complete their work, production teams are situated near the bottom of the fashion hierarchy. Lee and his colleagues are not considered to be artists or engineers, but rather a group of "workers." They are viewed as non-creative, replaceable "skilled labor" that merely follow instructions. Unjustifiably, professions deemed to be part of the working class are belittled by society. And in effect, the reward these professionals receive is limited and allocated based on their status.

According to scholastic philosopher and theologian St. Thomas Aquinas, the distribution of justice is determined by the individual's position in society; production teams are rewarded with little appreciation and acknowledgement for their creativity because they are considered to be part of the working class; whereas designers receive praise and recognition because they are positioned at the top of the fashion hierarchy (Capeheart & Milovanovic 2007: 14). While this unfair treatment and enforcement of a creative hierarchy cannot be blamed on any one figure or institution, it is acknowledged that there is an established system that determines the value and worth of one's professional/creative role. This accepted norm spans cross-culturally and through time, further situating Lee and his colleagues as non-creative beings.

Perhaps if our society was shaped more through political philosopher John Rawl's 'veil of ignorance'—where the fashion hierarchy and notions of one's position in society no longer existed—the inequality of creative acknowledgment would become balanced and Lee and others like him could become visible (Capeheart & Milovanovic 2007: 19).

Scholar Earl Tai argues that contrary to widespread belief, "design is not an esoteric luxury" but a universal desire and need (Tai 2009: 456). The pursuit and appreciation of aesthetics is not limited to the privileged, so why would the ability—creativity— to produce such designs and aesthetics be? Or if the designers practiced philosopher Peter Kropotkin's belief in solidarity as production teams do, maybe collective ownership could ensue. However, due to the nature of the fashion industry, the designers must follow the established model and attempt to have their sole name shining in the lights. The success of the designer relies on fabricating an image that reflects individual greatness. Attempting to share credit with production companies would do more damage than good to both parties. As Lee stated, if the designers are not successful, production companies lose clientele and will not be able to sustain themselves. Unfortunately, the established fashion system restricts designers from practicing Kropotkin's 'mutual aid' from coming into effect (Capeheart & Milovanovic 2007: 25). Either way, it is an unjust outcome.

While the scope of this case study is limited to the designers and garment district workers, the hierarchy of the fashion industry zooms out and encompasses many other players. Above the designers we find their marketing/ PR teams, investors, retailers, and Anna Wintour-esque figures. Below Lee and his cohorts is the labor force known as "sweatshop workers" and the impoverished outsourced labor that work under unimaginable conditions. A slight shift in focus on the rungs of the fashion ladder and we have another microcosm of injustice and new set of victims and perpetrators.

In a previous visit to Fine Line Production, Lee repeatedly stated that this is the "dark side of fashion." When asked to clarify, he shrugs his shoulders while giving a look of indifference and simply says, "No one knows about us. It's all behind-the-scenes (Lee 2012)." Lee agrees that the current system is unfair to garment district workers but assures me that he is perfectly happy and from his general impression, so are his colleagues (Lee 2012).

If "workers" were to claim their rights, how would the system respond? In a four year counterfeit lawsuit, seamstress Carmen Colle sued fashion powerhouse Chanel over a stolen crochet design. Colle claims Chanel rejected a proposed crochet design that was created by her team, World Tricot, but was later used in a Chanel collection and presented as their own. Colle was adamant in her claims and requested a combined total of 5.3 million for counterfeit and breach of contract damages (Davies 2011). At the conclusion of the lawsuit in 2009, the Paris court dismissed the counterfeit allegations, but awarded Colle with 400,000 for Chanel's breach of contract.

Colle's lawsuit was not simply about monetary compensation, but the right to be recognized as a creative being and to be seen as more than just a "resource to the designers (Passariello 2011)." While it is unknown if the crochet design was really a product of Colle's creativity or Chanel's, it is clear that contesting the system results in little reward.

Lee and many like him are not asking for shared fame, credit, or even increased appreciation, but rather the right to be visible, respected, and seen as creative beings—artists and engineers—to no longer be denied their existence and creativity.

IT'S
SEW
SAVE
THE
GARMENT
CENTER

Kelsey Allyn Glein

# Fashion Capital: Saving the Garment Center

New York City is arguably the fashion capital of the world. Unique from other cities, New York has been able to strike a balance between art and industry, allowing the city to transform into a center of fashion. The centrality of New York City's Garment District has allowed for the development of social and economic networks as well as an exchange of information through close physical proximity in the city's fashion industry (Rantisi 2006). Furthermore, it provides jobs for thousands of people and plays a role in keeping the local economy going. However, the Garment District is at risk of being torn apart completely, an injustice which would annihilate thousands of jobs through outsourcing and would arguably destroy part of the history of New York City. Though several factors including socio-economic trends and major political events contributed to New York City's rise to fashion fame, the Garment Center has allowed for New York to continue to thrive as the purported fashion capital of the world. According to Norma Rantisi, The New York Garment District was able to nurture a local design community and therefore "a distinct New York aesthetic that could stand apart from – and pose a formidable challenge to – Paris" (2006). However, at the start of the twenty-first century, the Garment District and fashion industry in New York City began to face new challenges in retaining New York's status as the fashion capital, in part because of the imminent decline of the Garment District as the spatial anchor for the industry (Rantisi 2006). New York City's Garment District is slowly being destroyed and taken over, and the jobs and its cultural significance are going with it, which coincides with a large trend of sending labor overseas where it can be done less expensively.

During this time of struggle for New York's Garment District comes Save the Garment Center (SGC), a trade association devoted to promoting New York's Garment District and the fashion companies and brands that use it. SGC attempts to "promote, preserve, and save New York City as fashion capital of the world" (SGC 2012). The initiative states that even though today only 5% of clothing sold in the United States was made in the United States, which is drastically down from 95% in 1960, there are still 846 fashion companies headquartered in New York City. This figure, they assert, is more than those in London, Paris, and Milan combined (SGC 2012). As a trade association, SGC supports factories, suppliers, and designers through education and advocacy for the Garment District in New York City. They purport that "the Garment Center is the soul of Midtown Manhattan, and the backbone of the NYC fashion industry" and that there is no other Garment Center in the world like New York's, which is why it must be saved (SGC 2012). The Garment District provides not only a space for creativity and a place for designers, but it provides jobs for everyone who contributes to the process of bringing fashion to life in New York City.

Save the Garment Center was started in 2007 as a grassroots campaign by factory owners Samanta Cortes, Anthony Lilore, Paul Cavazza and Larry Geffner. The campaign began as a response to City Hall's plans to lift the 1987 zoning laws that had protected the leases of the Garment Center fashion tenants for the past 23 years, but quickly developed into something more. In 2009, SGC became a 501c6 trade association and gained support from the Design Trust for Public Space and the Council of Fashion Designers of America through the creation of Made in Midtown, a study on the importance of New York City's Garment District. The campaign has made aware why the Garment District matters to fashion, and also why fashion matters to New York City. For the next phase of the project, the Design Trust for Public Space will facilitate public forums around the importance of creative industries in New York City. Then, the movement plans to work with all stakeholders to "generate strategies for zoning and land-use, to build city support for the fashion industry, and to develop programming or urban design initiatives that increase the industry's presence in the public realm" (Made in Midtown).

According to Save the Garment Center and Made in Midtown, the fashion industry and the Garment District are both an integral part of New York City's economy, identity, and sense of place (Made in Midtown). The Garment District has a crucial role not just in New York City, but also the United States, which is the why, according to Save the Garment Center, the "wrong" and injustice of its destruction must be addressed. This initiative states that is about more than fashion. It is "about one of the last neighborhoods in Manhattan that has not yet been remade by recent waves of new development. It's about jobs and immigrant workers. It's about the decisions city officials make to support certain kinds of businesses and land-use development, whether it's baseball stadiums, high-rise condominiums, or factories" (Made in Midtown). From the perspective of Save the Garment Center and Made in Midtown, justice will reign as long as New York City remains the fashion capital of the world and as long as the Garment District is preserved. The underlying "wrong" that SGC addresses is the loss of jobs in the Garment District and the invisibility of those who work there, but SGC does not explicitly state this at all. Seemingly, their perspective of "justice," though they do not specifically use the term, is one which saves and creates American jobs (there are 24,000 apparel manufacturing jobs in New York City), enables new fashion entrepreneurs to start a business and a fashion line, and prevents the Garment District from being moved out or shut down all together (SGC 2012).

This initiative to SGC attempts to preserve New York City as a place of fashion superiority. Underlying the major objectives of the project are the ideas that we are all players in the game of fashion, and that fashion is significant to both us individually and to the United States as a whole. Design scholar Earl Tai discusses the idea that aesthetics and design are imperative to how we succeed in life (Tai 2009: 456) and fashion theorist Joanne Entwistle has argued that fashion forms and shapes our identity (Entwistle 2000). What SGC is trying to achieve is to not only save a physical space, but to preserve and reinforce what that physical space represents: the power and significance of fashion in society. Rantisi states that "the history of New York fashion illustrates that it was the coming together of industrial and cultural activities that allowed for the dynamism, versatility and innovation of New York designs" with the Garment District as a central player (2006). In this case of justice, as Tai states, "design can be translated into economic value" with design taking place in the Garment District (Tai 2009: 457).

If social justice, as Loretta Capeheart and Dragan Milovanovic state, "is concerned not in the narrow focus of what is just for the individual alone, but what is just for the social whole" then Save the Garment Center, from a social justice perspective, could be seen as being concerned with what is just for New York City and the United States as a whole in regards to the economy, rather than the desires and attempts of particular individuals to profit from prime realty and space in Manhattan (2007: 2). SGC and Made in Midtown state that we must come together as a group to save the Garment District and that justice will not prevail if we continue to think and act only on our own behalf. Immanuel Kant theorized that the just state can only be realized by the collective will of the people, which a value this movement implies (Capeheart & Milovanovic 2007: 17). Max Weber speaks to the significance of individual responsibility in justice, particularly in a capitalist system (Capeheart & Milovanovic 2007: 34). Save the Garment Center is calling on individuals and groups, whether directly involved in the Garment District and fashion industry or not, to recognize the benefit and importance of New York City's Garment Center. The movement encourages "Made in NYC" and "Made in America" as a further statement that economic power and jobs are at stake, rather than just a physical space where fashion comes to life (SGC 2012).

However, it is worth questioning whether Save the Garment Center and the subsequent preservation of New York City as fashion capital is an issue of justice at all. Sociologist Max Weber once argued that highly privileged groups, in this case the leaders of the fashion industry, develop a myth of their natural superiority (Capeheart & Milovanovic 2007: 34). Has the Council of Fashion Designers of America, The Design Trust for Public Space, and Save the Garment Center exaggerated the importance of this physical space in Midtown Manhattan? It is possible that New York could retain its status of fashion capital without this physical space and cultural hub, though seemingly a piece of history would disappear if the Garment District was to shut down. Although SGC seemingly addresses the global injustice of outsourcing, they do not look at workers' right or workplace safety, which are inherently tied to the work that takes place in the Garment District. SGC would better solve injustice by addressing and incorporating these issues into their initiative. Paradoxically, many of the brands and designers fighting to save the Garment Center, both to enhance their public image and New York City's, are contributors to the outsourcing issue themselves. Seemingly, SGC does not directly address any type of injustice, as they ignore the crucial wrongs taking place through outsourcing while focusing on preserving the image of the fashion industry in New York City. Though, if this goes beyond fashion, if it is a fight for jobs, workers, and creativity, then Save the Garment Center reduces injustices through its advocacy. The fashion industry brings billions of dollars in yearly revenue to New York City, and the Garment District assists in making this cash flow possible (Made in Midtown). With "fast fashion" becoming the new paradigm for much of the fashion industry, the value of the design and production that takes place in the Garment District is invaluable.

An article in The New York Times asserts that many of the fashion production spaces and shops that once thrived in the Garment District have already been forced out (Bagli 2009). According to Charles V. Bagli, if fashion manufacturing in New York City is wiped out, the damage to the local economy is undeniable, as Fashion Week in September and February "attract enormous numbers of visitors and generate hundreds of millions of dollars in economic activity" (2009). Most of the manufacturing that takes place in the Garment Center is high-end, so it may not produce a large quantity of garments, but it produces a significant portion of total national sales. Owners of Garment District sewing rooms and factories are being forced to sublet or give up parts of their space and dispose of equipment they no longer have room for, causing them to cut back on workers and production (Bagli 2009). Seemingly, if they had more space, they believe they would be able to employ more workers and produce more garments. Nanette Lepore, a noted fashion designer who makes 80% of her clothing line in the Garment Center, states that if we fail to protect the Garment District today, young designers cannot survive, thousands of jobs will be lost, and that ultimately New York will not be the fashion capital of the world tomorrow (Bagli 2009).

As a project, SGC emphasizes Tai's ideas that design is important and must be included in discussions of justice as well as the importance of our physical environment in a capitalistic system (Tai 2009: 458). The fashion industry is valuable, both economically and culturally, and Save the Garment Center highlights this and aims to right the "wrong" of the Garment District's demise. However, Save the Garment Center seems to gloss over the issues of injustice that would occur in closing the Garment District, and they instead have created an "image" project to highlight New York City as a city of superior coolness over Milan, London, and Paris. Save the Garment seems to be an effort to maintain power and capital, rather than one to save jobs from going overseas. Does New York City need to remain the fashion capital of the world in order for justice to be served? Save the Garment Center and Made in Midtown would resoundingly answer "Yes!" and assert that the Garment District must remain intact for the sake of both art and industry in New York City and the United States. Beyond its current state of advocacy and awareness, it remains to be seen what Save the Garment Center and its major supporters like the Council of Fashion Designers of America will accomplish legally in saving this sacred space, the Garment District, that it outwardly representative of New York City's superior status in the world of fashion.

Laura Peach

# Victory Patterns: Sew your Heart Out...

Surrounded by neatly clipped hedges, two young women are seen playing in a contrived and posed way: taking their high-heeled shoes off to run, playing hide-and-seek, smiling in the sun. They are dressed in tie-dye tunic-like tops, which are how Victory Patterns articulates ethical fashion. The images are part of a fashion gallery on the Victory Patterns website to enhance the desirability and livability of the garments. Kristiann, the woman behind this small business, explains that "Victory Patterns came from a desire to create a responsible and ethically produced clothing line" when describing the project (Victory Patterns).

Her "user-friendly, fashionable, DIY-clothing line" provides patterns for women to sew their own clothing. Styles include sheer tops with asymmetrical hems, baby doll dresses with sweetheart necklines, and simple jersey jumpers. Required for engaging in this ethical mode of dress are the following: a printer and paper, to print off the pattern, which has to be pieced together, a sewing machine, and basic sewing skills. The patterns themselves, in PDF form, cost $10, and material for a simple dress is likely in the range of $15 to $45, depending on the textile.

The aesthetic clearly focuses on a young, fashion conscious woman, one with a slight hippy-vibe, based on the flowing textiles and tie-dye prints often used. These clothes seem made for casual play, not work environments. They also, by design, seem to favor a slender physique. By implication, the injustices that the "make your own clothing" camp seems to fight are the sweatshop labor at fast-fashion companies, which market similar designs. A sheer asymmetrical hem top could be purchased at Forever 21 this past season for under $10, and would take ten minutes to obtain. A woman creating a similar garment using Victory Patterns would spend three times that, and several hours in the production process.

Victory Patterns also obscures a social justice option in the other elements of dress that are needed to create a fashionable ensemble. The models in the fashion photograph are wearing leggings, jewelry and shoes that were likely not 'ethically' produced, but are rather mass market items. Where is the socially just jewelry? It seems that here, Victory Patterns is willfully turning a blind eye to the inherent contradictions. This bring up the need to articulate the nature of justice, which Greek philosopher Plato posits as the opposite of ignorance.

> What is the nature of injustice as compared with justice? For the statement made, I believe, was that injustice is a more potent and stronger thing than justice. But now, I said, if justice is wisdom and virtue, it will easily, I take it, be shown to be a stronger thing than injustice, since injustice is ignorance—no one could now fail to recognize that... (Plato 1989: 351)

In order to combat the projected, but un-named injustice of fast fashion, women move the labor of garment production back into their homes, paying a significantly higher price per garment. They believe that this method allows them to circumvent political philosopher Michael Sandel's fashion "vultures who prey on the desperation of others and are rewarded with windfall profits" (Sandel 2009: 7). But Sandel advocates for a just society as a culture where greed is punished, rather than rewarded. How do we differentiate between the greed of aesthetics and the greed of finance? In fact, the two greeds are feeding off each other: the woman's greed to look fashionable and keep up with the trends fuels the dangerous and sorrowful system of production that the greedy fashion corporation constructs.

Instead of producing more just fashion, perhaps Victory Patterns further administers what political artist Krzysztof Wodoczko's terms "painkillers of optimistic design fantasies" (Wodoczko 1999) by presenting an eden of alternative production without addressing the need for garment functionality or providing options for a broad and working social context. The amount of resources that a woman would need to put in in order to obtain a sheer asymmetrical hem top which will likely dissolve in aesthetic relevance in a three month period is disproportionate to the use value of the clothing.

Although in some ways, the patterns are an element in helping women with the capability to sew engage in current fashion trends. "Capability is a type of power" writes economist Amartya Sen, which is "a central concept in human obligation" (Sen 2008: 336). If we, as a society, were obliged to develop the capability to make our own clothes, then these patterns would provide an appropriate entry into the fashion system. But purchasing the patterns themselves does not give people the ability to put them to use.

In this Eden, only women of a certain demographic with resources to sewing machines and capabilities of sewing techniques can sew their hearts out and hold their heads high, knowing that at least their fashion-forward top was "ethically" made.

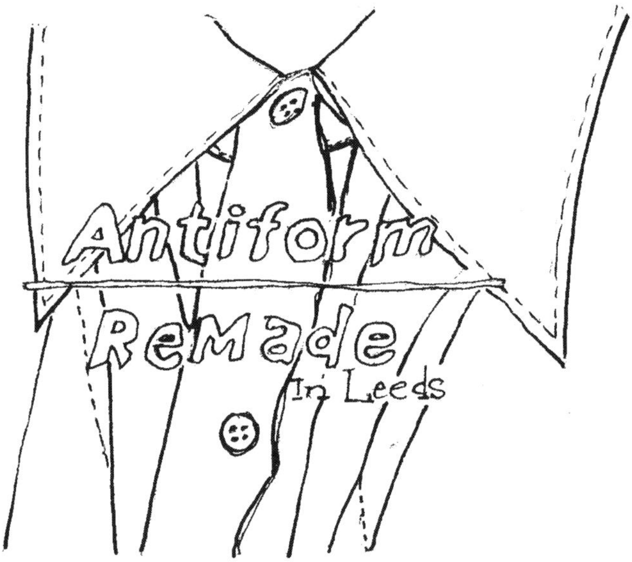
Antiform
ReMade
In Leeds

Alessandro Esculapio

# ReMade in Leeds Materializes Make Do and Mend

Fashion is generally regarded as an elitist phenomenon and the fashion system, although going through a process of democratization, is not inclusive. People are more often than not relegated to the role of mere consumers, something that prevents them from interacting with the material side of fashion, e.g. the garments themselves. These are the premises which allow concepts such as 'slow fashion' and 'critical consumption' to acquire growing importance in contemporary discourses on fashion. Clothing is only one of the many commodities that has been critically assessed recently, others being energy sources and food for instance. The shop ReMade in Leeds and the clothing line Antiform, both run by designer Lizzie Harrison, aim to promote and create awareness about such concepts.

The brand Antiform was established independently in 2007, while ReMade in Leeds began as a research project during Harrison's MA-studies at Fashion and Environment, London College of Fashion, in 2009. Whereas Antiform was created to promote issues of sustainability and ecology, ReMade in Leeds is a shop/creative space whose aim is to encourage people's participation in the design process and to have them engage with their clothes. The two projects are complementary and both serve as a tool to inform the public about alternative design and consumption practices.

## Antiform and Slow Fashion

The brand Antiform is committed to producing ecological designs and employing recycled or reclaimed materials as well as local ones. Knitwear, for example, is made according to the traditional Yorkshire knitting technique, a way to translate the idea of local production into a physical garment [1]. Antiform is a peculiar brand in that it is not limited to a sole typology of fashion design: it includes folk knits, vintage clothing, unique pieces and also a seasonal collection. The garments are sold online, both via Antiform's website and via popular retailers such as ASOS, in the shop ReMade in Leeds and in a few boutiques around the United Kingdom. The idea behind this pattern of distribution is that of reaching the widest possible audience, which may include people already engaged with sustainability at all levels, those who are aware of, say, organic food but not of 'organic' fashion, as well as consumers that lack knowledge of the field. One of Harrison's goals is in fact to promote sustainability among those who are not familiar with the concept: "It's important to take up the challenge of educating consumers who are not already sustainable shoppers, otherwise we're just talking to already informed people" (Harrison quoted in Krystle).

Another interesting initiative is the Antiform blog, accessible from the brand's website. The blog is a platform where the design team at Antiform can communicate and exchange ideas with the public. Through it, potential customers are informed on how garments are made and of which materials: a sort of history of clothes is created, so as to provide opportunity for emotional attachment, virtual sensory experience and understanding of the ideas behind the production. The blog also promotes and document the activities held at ReMade in Leeds, thus linking Harrison's projects and inviting people to be more than just consumers. The blog is a good example of effective alternative marketing in that it communicates the identity of the brand while at the same time overcoming the traditional patterns of producer/consumer.

As fashion designer Anne Theresia Wanders points out, telling the story of garments "can lead to greater identification with the product, so that the customer feels responsible for it and takes care of it longer" (Wanders 2009: 106-107). The internet has the potential to become what a couture atelier used to be: a place where customer and designer could fruitfully interact, where a personal attachment to the garment was created. This is one of the objectives of the so-called 'slow fashion' movement, a growing phenomenon that, in opposition to 'fast fashion' (the system that produces cheap mass goods), describes a sustainable attitude to design by producers and consumers alike. "In slow fashion emphasis is placed as much on reducing the speed of production as on slower consumption cycles. The consumer should identify with an article of clothing over the long term, feel more responsible for it, take care of it, treasure it. Producing less fashion, less frequently but of a higher quality is regarded as a means of preserving resources both in the production chain and in clothing care" (Wanders 2009: 89).

One aspect of slow and sustainable fashion that prevents it from becoming popular and accessible, though, is relatively higher prices for the garments, often motivated as inevitable when higher quality and fair practices are involved (Wander 2009: 93). Harrison, however, wishes to overcome this general belief: "I think a lot of sustainable fashion is aimed at people with quite a lot of money. People with money have choice whereas people without money don't have a huge amount of choice. I think we are defiantly raising awareness and I am really hoping that it is starting to raising awareness in areas of communities" (Harrison in Nicol).

Elitism in sustainable fashion could undermine its great potential and the principle of justice it tries to achieve and promote. The risk is clearly that of mimicking the patterns that already govern the traditional fashion system, thus excluding potential customers through the means of exclusivity. This goals is best exemplified by Harrison through her parallel project, ReMade in Leeds.

## ReMade in Leeds and Nussbaum's 'Capability Approach'

The shop/creative space ReMade in Leeds is more relevant in terms of community participation than its counterpart Antiform. Although clothes are sold here as in every other regular commercial space, it is not merely a boutique: courses and workshops are also offered. Harrison and her team host events like Leeds Community Clothes Exchange, dedicated to clothing swap, and workshops on sewing, machine knitting, textile upcycling and clothes mending. Such initiatives are a leap forward towards a more concrete democratization of fashion and clothing production, in that allows people to participate in the design process.

According to philosopher Martha Nussbaum, the 'Capability Approach' as a means to create social justice begins with two questions: "What are the people actually able to do and be? What real opportunities are available to them?" (Nussbaum 2006: x). So, when we consider fashion, the question we should ask is: what are people actually able to and be with garments and what opportunities are available to them in the fashion world? The fashion system we interact with nowadays (especially when considering the growing importance of 'fast fashion') is structured around the opposite roles of designer and customer. Through a 'capability approach' to fashion, it should be possible for people to participate not only as consumers; they should be accorded the capability to participate in other ways as well, depending on their personal inclinations.

Nussbaum describes capabilities as opportunities and abilities that should be guaranteed to everyone in a democratic society. "...the [capability] approach takes each person as an end, asking not just about the total or average well-being but about the opportunities available to each person. It is focused on choice and freedom, holding that the crucial good societies should be promoting for their people is a set of opportunities, or substantial freedoms, which people then may or may not exercise in action: the choice is theirs" (Nussbaum 2006: 18).

In fashion, then, this would mean giving people the choice to participate in the design process, for instance by allowing them the chance to personalize garments or by teaching them how to modify them. By allowing participants to acquire sewing skills, for example, Harrison and her team create for them the capability to mend and alter clothes. Whether they will decide to take advantage of these skills to repair, or even make, their own clothes or to keep buying new ones instead (perhaps from Antiform), that is a matter of personal choice.

Nussbaum proposes a list of fundamental capabilities that she calls 'central', capabilities that everyone should be able to exercise in a democratic system. One capability is that of "Sense, Imagination, and Thought", which also includes "being able to use imagination and thought in connection with experiencing and producing works and events of one's own choice, religious, literary, musical and so forth" (Alexander 2008: 64). We could then include the ability to design in the "so forth", arguing that the ability to take care of our own clothes and alter them is a manifestation of this specific capability. Could we also consider this a capability in a truly democratic fashion system, perhaps as the most important one? What other capabilities should be included in a democratic fashion system?

**Notes**

[1]. For a comprehensive history of local knitting traditions see Hartley, Marie (1951) *The Old Hand-Knitter of the Dales,* Dalesman Publishing.

remade in

LOUIS VUITTON

Minna Shim

# Practicing Interrogative Design: Slow and Steady Wins the Race

New York-based fashion designer Mary Ping launched her namesake label in 2001. The loose silhouettes, minimalistic detailing, and body conscious cuts of her collections stood out in the sea of over-glittered, obnoxiously loud, and poor quality designs of the ever-growing population of young designers. Her refreshing tastes and dedication to craftsmanship were immediately recognized and quickly garnered global interest; Ping was predicted to become the "next big thing." The young designer's career blossomed and she presented her collections repeatedly during NY Fashion Week and eventually in Paris—a grand feat for any designer (Granata 2009: 232).

Incorporating her philosophy into her aesthetics resulted in unique collections that simultaneously stimulated the senses and enlightened the mind. Ping's experience with the fast-paced nature of the fashion industry and observation of society's obsession with brand names inspired her to create Slow and Steady Wins the Race:

> Slow and Steady Wins the Race is a conceptual clothing and accessory line that reinterprets the classical everyday wardrobe. It is built on the belief that high design can be, and should be, accessible to all. Slow and Steady Wins the Race asks: What do we wear, why do we wear it, and how can we create new classics that are timely and timeless, unique yet universal? The work is a logical dissection of fashion, an investigation into the basic elements of what we wear, and a considered response to the hyper-consumerist pace of fashion (Slow and Steady Wins the Race).

Without sacrificing her aesthetics, Ping's Slow and Steady Wins the Race approaches design with integrity and the effort to provoke curiosity whilst making social commentary. Every Slow and Steady Wins the Race collection is presented as an exhibit-style still life, with little to no advertising. Slow and Steady Wins the Race is a rarity in the fashion industry; it breaks the mold of the "standard" designer where commercialism, consumerism, and branding are not the aim. Placing her eponymous label in hibernation for the past several years, Slow and Steady Wins the Race is the designer's main focus. The provocative, controversial, and unsettling qualities of Slow and Steady Wins the Race challenge the fashion industry and force us to reflect on our culture.

Social justice in terms of fashion calls for what artist Krzysztof Wodiczko refers to as interrogative design—design that "takes a risk, explores, articulates, and responds to the questionable conditions of life in today's world, and does so in a questioning manner" (Wodiczko 1999: 16). In her third Slow and Steady Wins the Race collection, Ping introduced her "alternate icon" bags (Granata 2009: 230). Resembling well known luxury handbags (e.g. Hermès' Birkin, Balenciaga's Motorcycle, Gucci's Classic, Bottega Veneta's Woven, and Chanel's Classic), Ping extracts recognizable features and integrates them into considerably less expensive fabrics and toned down designs which ultimately translates into a simpler and almost unfinished look.

By targeting identifiable luxury goods and 'deconstructing' its characteristics, Ping is examining the "processes of consumption and their association with class and taste, forcing us to pause and contemplate, perhaps even question, why and how we consume what we do" (Granata 2009: 231). Ping is attempting to address the inequality of class and the influential role luxury goods play in determining status and the economic hierarchy of our society.

While not all of her pieces are considered scandalous or imbued with social commentary, Ping's designs are characteristically non-mainstream. By purposefully limiting the production of her designs, "creating non-seasonal pieces, and containing the price...the designer is also intent, in her very small way, to slow down the fashion cycle and 'counter fashion's in-built obsolescence" (Granata 2009: 231).

It can be argued that this combination of humor and reappropriation as a form of social commentary produces a more personal and stronger sense of self-reflection. By consciously purchasing an object that can be simultaneously practical and make a statement, the consumer is choosing to be constantly reminded of what the "alternate icon" bag symbolizes; implying that there is a deeper understanding and connection to the motive of the design.

The use of agency by Ping is also important to note. According to philosopher Cornelius Castoriadis, "societies are self-creative and yet most... are utterly incapable of calling into question their own established norms" (Garner 2011). Ping is challenging the heteronomy enforced by luxury companies and using her autonomy to challenge and reappropriate iconic bags to question our society (Garner 2011).

However, is Ping's re-appropriation of luxury goods really accomplishing anything? Or are her actions just resulting in the creation of another substitute designer good? The "alternate icon" bags are as artist Krzysztof Wodiczko encourages, "attracting while scandalizing...and [accomplishing] a performative articulation" (Wodiczko 1999: 17). Yet, isn't this mockery and judgmental pointing of fingers only fueling a new fashion obsession for obtaining Ping's "non-brands" and niche items? Is this quiet attack on luxury brands a fair and just way to execute interrogative design?

Interrogative design should also "secure a vision for a better future" (Wodiczko 1999: 16). The unequal accessibility of fashion is considered unfair and unjust. The current fashion system is based on a socio-economic hierarchy where high designs are unattainable to those on the bottom rungs of the economic ladder. Slow and Steady Wins the Race's manifesto purports that "high design can be, and should be, accessible to all" (Slow and Steady Wins the Race)—implying that a democratization of fashion is needed in today's society. Well designed and high quality goods should be available to everyone, regardless of class.

However, Ping's method of limiting the production of her goods doesn't slow fast fashion, but rather creates an exclusivity that prevents participation—producing a niche market. This intentional scarcity of goods results in the increase of what economist Fred Hirsch labels as a "snob value" (Ellis & Heath 1983: 7). In 2009, Ping was interviewed by Professor Francesca Granata where snobbery was addressed:

> FG: I was also thinking of how people who are wearing brands in the form of a luxury bag, whether original or not, are trying to appropriate a symbolic capital and an association with wealth. Yet in some ways, the bags you make also have their symbolic capital, as well as perhaps a cultural capital which makes them a little bit more snobbish. They are saying that their wearers don't need a luxury bag and that they know fashion enough to be able to play with it.
>
> MP: Yes, maybe there is an intellectual snobbery to those who are wearing the bag, or end up purchasing the bag. Although for the most part, I think the people who buy it share the same sense of humor. They have their own opinion of what these status bags are, and they own or they could probably own one of them, but it goes back to having a sense of humor and perhaps making a subtle statement about something that's going on within our consumer culture (Granata 2009: 235).

Ping's attempts at challenging notions of class are also undermined by the prices of her goods. A jean Hermès reappropriation costs $150.00 while a leather reappropriation costs over $1,000.00—prices that compete with luxury items. The "alternate icon" bag collection addresses our culture's desire for luxury brands and obsession with display, but by criticizing our society in this manner doesn't achieve the desired outcome. Ping's designs become a tool for exclusivity and judgment and, in effect, create another hierarchy of intelligence and class, almost implying that purchasing and carrying a real Hermès, Chanel, or Gucci is inferior.

Maybe if Ping's bags were of no cost or truly available to all and unlimited, maybe it would then make a more effective statement and support the democratization of fashion. Mary Ping's Slow and Steady Wins the Race attempts to provoke, challenge, and ultimately change our society for the better. While there is no way of measuring the impact and effectiveness of her work, it can not be denied that her "alternate icon" bag creates a much needed discussion—which according to Wodiczko—is the intent of interrogative design (Wodiczko 1999: 16).

THE GREEN SHOWS

Maureen Brewster

# The GreenShows: Eco-chic or Just a Show?

The eco-couture movement has over the last decade been gaining ground, and retailers from H&M to Gucci have leapt on-board, creating lines touting sustainable fabrics, low-impact production techniques, and more. Vogue notes that green fashion has traveled far from its humble "hippie hemp-sack origins" to enter new, haute territory, with designers like Stella McCartney and Martin Margiela contributing to the rise of eco chic (Vogue 2012). A disconnect remains, however, between niche labels such as these with the wider couture industry; in any fashion line-up, environmentally conscious labels are distinctly outnumbered. At New York Fashion Week, for example, these design houses are typically ostracized to entirely separate presentations that are unaffiliated with the main event. Enter The GreenShows (TGS), a "premier event management and marketing company dedicated to the ethical and sustainable luxury fashion and lifestyle movement" (TGS 2012). Prizing an ethical and sustainable approach to producing, disseminating, and consuming fashion, TGS has developed a range of strategies to realize their goal of connecting eco-literate consumers with a more socially and environmentally just fashion industry.

The idea that social and environmental justice are tightly bound is implicit; as social theorists Loretta Capeheart and Dragan Milovanovic point out, for social justice "issues of fairness and quality of life are interconnected" (Capeheart & Milovanovic 2007: 96), thus making access to a healthy, sustainable environment a growing part of the social justice initiatives around the world. The difference here is that TGS, however minute a platform, brings fashion into this equation; in doing so, they have helped to introduce a much-needed dialogue which resonates with the imperative of social justice to engage with "nature, harm, and humanity" (Capeheart & Milovanovic 2007: 94). TGS aims to address these issues within the fashion system, and have begun to receive recognition for their work by the industry at large. After being included in New York's Fashion Week for the first time this past fall, TGS is gaining visibility for its strategy of merging a green ethos with a commercial enterprise, but this act may be a hard one to follow. The company is very clear about its stringent set of standards for prospective designer collaborators: among others, it requires fair labor policies; a "slow-fashion" approach based on customized, community-centered production; low-impact, natural materials; even an emphasis on sustainable and socially aware marketing practices (The GreenShows 2012).

These guidelines set TGS apart from an industry that has been characterized by its incomplete compliance with ethically and ecologically sound principles. Many brands, couture and big-box retailers alike, have been able to ride the wave of consumer desire for eco-fashion by cherry-picking the criteria that best fits their bottom line, with the end result being little more than a few half-truths printed on a garment's label. The U.S. Federal Trade Commission (FTC) has recently revised environmental marketing guidelines, which it acknowledges are necessary to mitigate the often misleading claims of environmental friendliness that are "nearly impossible to substantiate" by companies hoping to entice consumers; however, there remain several grey areas not resolved by the FTC's report, namely surrounding the terms 'sustainable' and 'natural,' which cannot be adequately substantiated due to their lack of definitive meaning ("F.T.C. Issues Guidelines for 'Eco-Friendly' Labels," The New York Times, 2012).

Though it remains to be seen how the changes proposed by the report will affect the production and consumption of the fashion industry as a whole, the very need for a more comprehensive evaluative process indicates that TGS' policies are ahead of the curve. The company is in fact identifying and attempting to rectify a void in the current eco-fashion trade: the necessity for quantification of claims of ethical and sustainable production, and also to create a means of connecting conscious consumers with responsible labels. Unlike many other businesses, which often "greenwash" their products by not fully accounting for all aspects of its production and consumption (TerraChoice 2007), the TGS standards provide a thorough rubric for each of their collaborators- and mindful consumers- to evaluate and follow. In short, their business model indirectly addresses two injustices in the fashion system: the many socially and environmentally reprehensible operational practices within the industry, and the lack of consumer access to verifiably ethical and eco-friendly goods.

Having built such a strong scrupulous foundation within their commercial goals, TGS can be examined in comparison with the philosophy of Immanuel Kant (1724-1804): specifically his ideas of moral duty. Kant writes that humanity is comprised of "rational beings, capable of reason… independent of nature or inclination" (Sandel 2009: 118). This in turn makes us capable of moral discretion, and the ability to understand the difference between our competing motives of duty and inclination. Sandel continues that "any and all attempts to satisfy our wants, desires, preferences and appetites" would be classified as motivated by inclination; only "doing something because it's right, not because it's useful or convenient" would constitute an action performed from a motive of duty, which is the only one that confers moral worth as defined by Kant (112). Central to Kant's moral philosophy is an emphasis on human dignity and universal rights; TGS, with its clearly defined code of ethics and sustainability, references Kant's views on the connection between morality, social justice, and freedom as it urges a more socially just fashion system.

However, TGS is a fashion marketing and event management company, and therefore arguably leans toward motives of inclination by staging fashion shows and the like. They make no secret of their goal to provide a pleasurable, fashionable experience: as TGS partner and fashion designer Lara Miller said, "We're creating genuine ideas, and those genuine ideas do have a compassionate aspect to them; but first and foremost they are fashion-forward, stylish, smartly-styled pieces" (Inhabitat 2009). The fact that TGS has not extended its reach past satisfying these motives of inclination problematizes a purely benevolent reception of the GreenShows business model. Though its adherence to a strict code of conduct in regards to the ethical treatment of the environment, producers and consumers speaks to a motive of duty and confers some moral worth upon their work, there is no indication of plans to initiate change on a broader level, or to disrupt the current system in any way. Their model of using only small, eco-couture labels in exclusive events also restricts participation, limiting access to those who are socioeconomically disadvantaged, and would be difficult to translate for a wider demographic. TGS is therefore much more successful, albeit on a very small scale, at countering the greenwashing of the fashion industry than they are at improving access to ecologically and ethically responsible goods. Their underdeveloped attempt unfortunately makes for an uncomfortable resemblance to the practices of the very system they are supposedly seeking to counter.

Having moved from operating alongside New York Fashion Week to becoming a featured component certainly signals a victory the GreenShows– and for socially and environmentally conscious fashion on the whole– but it remains to be seen how this will impact the entrenched apathy of the fashion industry towards altering its practices. As eco-couture evolves and grows, it will become more important than ever to define the hazy terms that have attached themselves to the movement, and the fashion system would do well to use The GreenShows' strategy of incorporating style and substance as a starting point for more progressive change. The fashion system is beginning to recognize the need to be mindful of the ethics and sustainability of its producers and products, and though at the present time TGS' model has yet to reach its full potential, it is a marked start towards the change that increasingly eco-literate consumers are calling for. Ideally the fashion system will become, as Kant philosophizes, a "kingdom of ends" (Capeheart & Milovanovic 2007: 17) in which every rational, socially conscious fashion consumer recognizes the impact of their sartorial choices, the absolute value of the human and environmental components that created them, and develops a system of laws bound by a unified will to make socially and environmentally just fashion.

TIFFANY & CO.

Minna Shim

# Charity for Breakfast: The Tiffany & Co. Foundation

Established in 2000, "The Tiffany & Co. Foundation's mission is to protect the beauty of nature and the creativity of human nature" (The Tiffany & Co. Foundation). By providing grants to nonprofit organizations and supporting various initiatives, The Tiffany & Co. Foundation sets out to encourage environmentally friendly actions and enhance the field of design and art (The Tiffany & Co. Foundation).

Focusing on four "program areas"—responsible mining, coral conservation, urban parks, and excellence in design—most of The Tiffany & Co. Foundation's philanthropic endeavors align with their business interests. Since 2000, The Tiffany & Co. Foundation has awarded close to $47 million to different organizations/initiatives in the varying program areas. With strict guidelines and rules for eligibility, "grants are awarded by The Tiffany & Co. Foundation board of directors who meet twice annually" (The Tiffany & Co. Foundation).

The conception of The Tiffany & Co. Foundation is in part a result of Tiffany & Co.'s strong belief in corporate responsibility. As a leader of luxury and an influential fashion powerhouse, Tiffany & Co. believes it is their "moral imperative to sustain the natural beauty that inspires their designers, customers, and employees" (Tiffany & Co.).

Luxury and philanthropy are seldom viewed in the same light; and in the rare occasions they are, skepticism lingers right around the corner—as if something deceptive is lurking beneath the gloss of artifice. Perhaps this cynicism stems from the interlinking of fashion charity with consumerism and branding, e.g., Donna Karen's Urban Zen, Gap's (RED) collection, or any of Diane von Furstenberg's highly publicized charitable donations. Philosopher Slavoj Žižek argues that in today's capitalistic structure, the performance of purchasing something as a form of humanitarianism has become an accepted norm. According to Žižek, our altruistic duties have become "included in the price" of whatever object or idea we are "buying into," essentially we are "redeeming" philanthropy with consumerism. This becomes problematic because it "degrades and demoralizes" the ethics of charity (Žižek 2009).

While it is naïve to think that the intentions of The Tiffany & Co. Foundation are pure and selfless or even that their endeavors have brought about great change—it is important to note that their approach differs from the common fashion charity: they don't ask their consumers to purchase something as a form of charitable giving, nor does The Foundation ask for any sort of monetary donation or set forth fundraising initiatives.

Although The Foundation is officially called The Tiffany & Co. Foundation, the incorporation of branding is minimal compared to the other brand-laden fashion charities. Yes, the same Tiffany blue can be found on The Foundation's website and yes, The Foundation receives its financial endowment from their mother company—so basically from consumer purchases—however, The Foundation acts largely as a separate entity from their Tiffany & Co. counterpart by excluding product placement and any mention of the consumer as a donor, which is a stark contrast to the established norms of fashion philanthropy. On the other hand, it may be viewed that their approach of indirect branding vs. direct branding in effect, accomplishes the same outcome: consume for charity.

In the "Corporate Responsibility" section of Tiffany & Co.'s website, they offer an in-depth explanation of their philosophy and initiatives as a "responsible corporation." They discuss the integrity of their business practices and mention little of The Foundation, again implying that they function as separate charity units. However, product placement was not lacking in this platform; a plethora of thematic jewels can be found throughout the Tiffany & Co.'s "Corporate Responsibility" section. Clearly, Tiffany & Co. and The Foundation have different approaches to their philanthropic endeavors. Or do they?

Economist and philosopher Amartya Sen argues that we should not strive for a just society, but rather a more just society, namely by using the "human development approach…a call to action, of the responsibility of people to bring about…change…if someone has the power to make a change that he or she can see will reduce injustice in the world…" (Sen 2008: 335). Sen furthers his argument by quoting Buddha: "He [Guatama Buddha] argued that since we are enormously more powerful than the other species, we have some responsibility towards other species…" and without regard for the benefits or rewards one can gain from their philanthropic actions (Sen 2008: 336-337). Is The Foundation fulfilling their responsibility as a privileged, capable, and powerful force?

The Tiffany and Co. website thoroughly outlines their corporate responsibility and the ethical actions they take when procuring the minerals needed to sustain their business; the mining of metals, diamonds, and gemstones and the use of leather, coral, and paper goods are addressed. It seems all aspects of their procurement practices are conducted in an eco-friendly and sustainable manner. "Recognizing that unsustainable coral harvesting can damage critically important marine ecosystems, and that many coral species face a variety of threats, Tiffany & Co. has refused to use coral in our jewelry since 2002" (Tiffany and Co.). While this step is admirable and exemplary, the elimination of coral in Tiffany and Co. designs may not solely be about preserving the environment; compared to other minerals such as gold, diamonds, and gemstones, designs with coral are less popular and result in fewer profits. Eliminating coral from their collections doesn't hurt their business and helps with branding themselves as a responsible corporation. Tiffany and Co. also attempts to use sustainable mining practices for other minerals such as silver, gold, and platinum:

> In Fiscal Year 2011, Tiffany & Co. purchased the silver used in our own manufacturing facilities from two U.S. sources. 69%* of this silver was sourced from the Bingham Canyon Mine in Utah as a by-product of an open-pit copper mine. The remaining 31%* was procured from recycled sources. In Fiscal Year 2011, Tiffany & Co. purchased the gold used in our own manufacturing facilities from two U.S. sources. 48%* of this gold was sourced from the Bingham Canyon Mine in Utah as a by-product of an open-pit copper mine. The remaining 52%* was procured from recycled sources, up from 36% in 2010. The Bingham Canyon Mine is an existing mine that produces gold as a by-product of copper mining using a non-cyanide [emphasis added] leaching extraction method. While there are legacy environmental issues from over a century of mining at Bingham Canyon, the mine's owners deserve recognition for acting responsibly and aggressively to address these issues. In Fiscal Year 2011, Tiffany & Co. purchased the platinum used in our own manufacturing facilities from three U.S.-based companies. 55%* of this platinum was sourced from known mines in the United States, the majority from Stillwater Mining in Montana. The remaining 45% was procured from a U.S.-based refiner which sources platinum from a mixture of mined and recycled sources (Tiffany and Co).

Scholar John M. Alexander provides an analysis of Sen's critique. According to Alexander, Sen claims "the idea that people look out for their self-interest and welfare is only partially true...people also genuinely care about their community...and not out of their egoistic interest but in the interest of those they care about" (Alexander 2008: 21). Not only is The Tiffany & Co. Foundation feeling "sympathy" but also executing "commitment" (Alexander 2008: 21).

Regardless of the sincerity and integrity of The Tiffany & Co. Foundation or the rewards received by their endeavors, the question that comes to mind is: Does the nature of The Foundation's initiatives become unethical if they are in fact receiving corporate gain?

The Foundation advocates responsible mining and "believes that the manner in which precious metals and gemstones are extracted is of the utmost importance...and values healthy oceans and the important role that corals play in the ecosystems...and believes that precious corals cannot be sustainably removed from the oceans for use in jewelry or home décor" (The Tiffany & Co. Foundation). Urban parks, such as the High Line received $6 million from The Foundation and consequently named a portion of the park The Tiffany & Co. Foundation Overlook (The Tiffany & Co. Foundation). Is Tiffany & Co. really practicing their corporate responsibility, or are they as Žižek says, "...simply repairing with their right hand what they ruined with their left" (Žižek 2009)?

Laura Peach

# Locating Liberated Dress in Local Wisdom

The Local Wisdom project collects stories of individuals who engage in alternative dress codes and wearing practices in cities such as London, Oslo, Berlin and San Francisco, and posts them on a online forum to provide readers with models of a new way of thinking about their relationship with their clothing. Many of these dress codes and wearing practices revolve around the traditions of re-use and wearing garments that belonged to family members as a form of liberated dress. The project, started by Dr. Kate Fletcher and funded by a private grant in the UK, "aims to challenge the dependency of the fashion industry on increasing material output and propose solutions through sustained attention to tending and using garments, not just creating them" (Local Wisdom 2012).

Though there are many methods that the project highlights in order to achieve this goal, it is surprising how many of the stories center around personal histories and an ethos of continuity through garments which had a history behind them. One girl wears the denim jacket that was worn for many years by both of her older brothers; she appreciates the way in which the fold on the collar has become threadbare. Another young woman loves wearing the jumpsuit that marked her grandmother as fashionable in the 1970s. A young man connects emotionally with the type of person that his grandfather was when wearing his jacket (Local Wisdom 2012).

Fashion theorist Elizabeth Wilson writes that "liberated dress, according to the [feminist] ideology, means 'doing your own thing'" (Wilson 2007: 237). Wilson quotes a woman from a British newspaper who self-righteously touts herself as being outside of the "distant, non-sensical world of fashion," since she wears the same summer frocks three years in a row and a sweater knitted by her mother when it's chilly (Wilson 2007: 236). This seems to fall in line with many of the personalities featured on the Local Wisdom project, in so far as being outside the fashion system and embodying a form of liberated dress. And yet, there is something more here. It is not just that these garments continue because of their inherent material qualities:

textile, cut, color, shape, but rather that they have a story which creates an emotional connection between the first, second, and third wearer: these are garments with histories.

Economist Amartya Sen says that the question of justice is not so much "whether everyone will act according to what they see as reasonable... but what exactly they should see as reasonable, and for what particular reason" (Sen 2008: 335). How do we challenge or shift notions of what is reasonable when it comes to dressing? How does re-wearing an item that belonged to a family member become somehow a more reasonable fashion presentation than simply shopping in a thrift store? Why do we hold on to the clothing of the ones closest to us? Perhaps with memory, comes responsibility.

The Local Wisdom project also provides a way for individuals to challenge the established fashion system, to voice their divergent modes of wearing and creation of styles. It is similar in structure to the newsmedia project that sociologist Carl Jensen started in order to take stories that were not given weight and coverage by the traditional newsmedia, and put them on the public's radar. His Project Censored publishes an annual list of the 25 most censored news stories on topics like the business of private prisons. By bringing to light such topics, both projects work to find a way to emancipate the public from the Liberation Sociologists Joe Feagin and Hernan Vera explain that "everyday life is an interaction, with most people coming into contact with others everyday. Every human being's life is shaped by social contacts...[which are] expressed in informal networks" (Feagin & Vera 2001). The ways in which Local Wisdom allows individuals to express memory and practice re-use though clothing shifts the power of fashionablity in the informal networks where people interact with eachother in everyday life.

Perhaps, if there were a way to infuse the fashion system with more memory, if projects like Local Wisdom became incorporated on a wider scale, the fashion system, as it is internalized and practiced in everyday life, might begin making steps towards a more real action of sustainability, through conservation and creativity in reviving and reinterpreting already-existing garments in a current context. Then we may begin to compose wardrobes that resonate with individual identities which also approach the horizon of a just world.

POST-

# SCRIPT

Otto von Busch

# Fashion, Democracy and Social Justice

Justice concerns the issues of rightness, fairness and equity. As noted by philosopher John Rawls, "Justice is the first virtue of social institutions, as truth is of systems of thought." (Rawls 1999: 3) It is the foundation on which society is built. Justice is also intimately connected to the political, as politics is the distribution of social relationships, the private and public, authority and power. Legal philosopher Ronald Dworkin advances the idea that equality is at the core of every political theory (Dworkin 1977: 179ff). Justice is something happening between us everyday too, even if it is most often represented in relation to social institutions and systems such as property, labor, government, and especially, the execution of power. But in fashion we do not often discuss issues of power or justice, even though fashion seeps into our lives from every corner. Fashion, just like beauty, is not democratic or fair. It is distributed unequally among people.

Most often we can pass through our everyday life without noticing the question of justice. It is something that is exposed when we notice something "wrong", something disturbing, a polemical point, or an injustice. To philosopher Jacques Rancière this is where the political is exposed to us: we suddenly notice that someone is uncounted or excluded, and a social "wrong" is being exposed (cf. Rancière 2004). As Rancière points out, this "wrong" is not a juridical one as there are not two recognized or determined parties. One of them is unseen, unaccounted for. We thus need to mobilize our sensibilities in order to perceive the injustice that is before us. From this perspective, at the core of democracy is the demarcation of who is the subject, who is counted as citizen, who can vote, who is seen and who has a say. Politics is about the distribution of recognition as equals, not only in a juridical way, but from the sensible itself. From the perspective of fashion we need to recognize that we are neck-deep in an abyss of injustices and find ways to address these issues.

Just like fashion, also our perception of what is a "wrong" shifts with the times. Great philosophers, like Aristotle, have made contributions to the philosophy of justice, yet they were blind to injustices such as slavery and women's rights. We are still partly blind, as issues of racism, child labor and equal pay for equal work are still issues under debate. In fashion, sweatshops have been discussed since the birth of the industrial revolution, yet they are left unresolved or simply moved beyond our immediate sight. However, sweatshops are just one facet of the social injustices executed through fashion.

One of the key paradoxes of fashion is perceived equality. We can all dress fashionably – if we have the money, that is. That is why the social impact of fast and cheap fashion over the last decade has been so powerful, and has also become such a great varnish over the deteriorating social landscape around us. Perhaps most perplexing is how the success of cheap fashion, as well as other forms of consumerism, has in the west managed to divert the attention from other urgent socio-political issues for a whole generation. Young people today can buy a lot more consumer goods and clothes than their parents could. Yet at the same time, few recognize that their real income level, and the possibilities for social progress, seem darker than a generation ago. Political issues, such as job security, the possibility to own a house, or having a future pension, seem to have disappeared from the everyday agenda. Simultaneously, consumer democracy in the form of cheap goods are the politics of the day and it is on this arena we fight tooth and claw. The "social" is something we choose to consume, rather than commit to or build strong and lasting relationships through. As our sociality is becoming expressed also digitally through "friends", "followers" and "fans", the ephemeral image culture of fashion likewise seems a perfect fit for our time's social relations.

Fashion shapes a certain form of sociality. It opens up ways of belonging that bypass some of the social distinctions of ethnicity, education or class. We can dress to become the one we want to become, or to be seen as. Simultaneously, as sociologist Pierre Bourdieu famously proposed, we also use fashion to produce distinctions to mark out the borders between socio-economic and cultural groups (Bourdieu 1984). The community, culture or subculture we dress distinctly to belong to is shaped in a similar way as Benedict Anderson's idea of nations being "imagined communities" (Anderson 1983). As Anderson suggests, the sociality of nations is created, not primarily by everyday relations or inheritance, but by the mental image of shared affinity. This image is projected through media and enacted in events and rituals in order to build a social fabric and national loyalty beyond the social, "conceived as a deep, horizontal comradeship." (Anderson 1983: 224)

Today's "democratized" fashion, so cheap and abundant that it seems accessible to everyone, exhibits a similar illusion of "horizontal comradeship". We dress as our peers, yet also strive to keep some traces of individuality. Any style is possible, every subculture is a commodity, everything is accessible to anyone, at least as copies. We feel *we have the power* to become part of fashion. Yet the mechanism of fashion commodities only conforms to the power of the dominant mode of production; the consumer can "vote" with their money, and we feel involved, but at the same time we cannot participate. As the fashions change, we think we can take part in a deeper change, but the shift happens only on the surface. As philosopher Jean Baudrillard notes on consumerism: "to the illusion of change is added the illusion of democracy." (Baudrillard 1981: 78) The "democratization" may instead fuel an increasing social stress or status anxiety. (de Botton 2004) The fashion system simultaneously liberates and imprisons: as noted by fashion historian Anne Hollander, "the tyranny of fashion itself has in fact never been stronger than in this period of visual pluralism." (Hollander 1993: 345)

Yet the tyranny of fashion is not an obvious one – we are not forcibly oppressed through violent intimidation. To most of us, fashion leaves no physical bruises. But still we are coerced, controlled and affected, or drawn by the cleverly designed systems of desire that are part of consumerism, and in which fashion plays a central role. Fashion can, in this sense, be part of "democracy incorporated", an image of our liberal democracies advanced by political philosopher Sheldon Wolin (2008). To Wolin, this is a society that expresses totalitarian tendencies through an "obsession with control, expansion, superiority, and supremacy." (Wolin 2008: ix) In what Wolin calls an "inverted totalitarianism", the political demobilization of the citizenry through consumer society is combined with a decentralized domination through economic influence over state politics. While the fashion industry may have little power over governance and state politics, it may still play a crucial role in the desire-driven demobilization of consumers, while simultaneously celebrating the subject's illusionary individualism and autonomy. In its apparent pluralism and perceived equality, fashion provides a perfect illustration of incorporated consumerism and what Wolin describes as a "managed democracy" where power is legitimated through controlled elections and voters are as "predictable as consumers" (Wolin 2008: 47). This is the duping of the people through a micro-management that is far removed from a general and self-reflective participation in self-government, which leaves citizens without real power.

Activist and scholar Frances Moore Lappé has proposed that in consumer society most of us are trapped in a "spiral of powerlessness" where we, in our detached state, are discouraged to engage in the ruling of the world (Lappé 2010). In media we are met with the proponent images of the "survival of the fittest" and man's autonomous selfishness, and thus we come to distrust our fellows and government. As Lappé notices, the more powerless we are, the more fearful, and the more we ask for help and external salvation. Instead for turning to each other for help, we turn against each other and direct our hope to the "magic market" which can make us individually wealthy and safe. But as wealth is concentrated, most often to individuals on top of us, it warps politics and increases injustice, making us feel even more powerlessness. "Feeling powerless, we're robbed of energy and creativity, with hearts left open to fear, despair and depression." (Lappé 2010: 4)

In a similar vein, activist and theorist Michael Lerner addresses the issue of what he calls "surplus powerlessness" (1986). While real powerlessness is the result of oppression and inequities by systems or other people, surplus powerlessness is an internalized submission and continuous feeling of hopelessness. Those who have felt powerless for an extended length of time tend to accept conditions in the world they would otherwise reject. This emotional capitulation is an apathy that shies away from struggle, in the belief that nothing can ever change for the good. The activist may be working for a just cause, or even create a great opportunity and make advances in the struggle, but a mindset of powerlessness takes the edge off any possible agency. Economist Amartya Sen has called this "adaptive preferences" and finds it a common attitude of impairment among people who live in deprived conditions where "hardship is accepted with non-grumbling resignation" and they "take pleasure in small mercies and [...] cut down personal desires to modest – 'realistic' – proportions" (Sen 1992: 55). This can for example be the case of exploited migrants, battered housewives, or oppressed minorities.

This embodied powerlessness can be found on many levels and among many groups in society. In a survey on people with disabilities, social psychologist Adrienne Asch found that "[the disabled] have seen the problems as inherent in their medical conditions and have not been urged to join others to demand structural changes that would render the environment useful for them." (Asch 1986: 13) Thus the disabled in her study accepted injustice and inequitable treatment as something "human", something unquestionable, and not an issue for which to demand equity and social justice. One way of convincing people that change is impossible is to make them believe that they are atomized individuals, that they control the production of their identity, or that they can't trust anyone else but themselves.

Today's current, fast, and relatively accessible, paradigm of mass-produced fashion is said to be for all. The brand Uniqlo even has the slogan "Made for all" in their ads. But their stores are not where the poor live. Sizing and models are racially stereotyped and homogenized. People are still excluded, uncounted and unseen. As suggested by Rawls, the center of social justice is the concern to improve the conditions of the least advantaged members in society, rather than just to maximize the general social welfare. That means that even if cheap fashion is produced for the masses, as long as it does not seriously improve the conditions of the sweatshop workers, the disabled, or the poor, then this change is worth nothing.

Yet "democracy" in fashion today has another agenda; that of mass-homogenization. It is something former magazine editor Michele Lee has called "McFashion": as unsatisfying, commonplace and utterly forgettable as the fast food equivalent (Lee 2003). This type of mass dissemination of goods not only fails to satisfy the desire of people, it also raises the level of competition and thus fuels even greater patterns of consumptions – or what we could call "fashion obesity".

Highlighted in the 1970's by Fred Hirsch, this is also a core dilemma of liberal democracies, something he called the "social limits of growth" (Hirsch 1977). To Hirsch, in society we strive for both performance and position. It can be goods, education, jobs and the social respect they bring. Yet, "as the average level of consumption rises, an increasing portion of consumption takes on a social as well as an individual aspect." (Hirsch 1977: 2) Not only do we come to spend a higher proportion on "positional goods" which aim to raise our social standing, but this act also comes to pollute the social environment like exhaust from cars pollutes the natural world. Mass-production of positional goods continually elevates the threshold of our contentment. We are continuously unsatisfied, even though we spend more and more. The social realm becomes congested with upward-striving individuals and the value of our positional goods keeps deteriorating. Not only our roads are congested – also our social space. Fashion Avenue is not so glamorous as we first may think, but rather congested and polluted by what Hirsch calls "social waste" (Hirsch 1977: 6), caused by our decaying positional goods.

In the period after the Russian revolution, legal scholar Evgeny Pashukanis pointed out how Marx's concept of "commodity fetishism" also has come to influence our legal institutions (Pashukanis 2003). Commodity fetishism transforms human values and relations into commodities and objectified economic relationships where every agent is identified either as buyer or seller. Money becomes the objective standard to compare labor and objects, effectively hiding the different relations and situations from which the commodities emerged. Money becomes the "universal equivalent" masking the memory of human values: "Quality has been changed into quantity, substance into form, and money is now worshipped as the universal equivalent." (Pashukanis 2003: xxi) As Pashukanis shows, a similar mechanism is also the basis for our legal formats where "formal equality" is the universal equivalent for our concept of justice.

The issue addressed by Pashukanis by this transposition of Marx's idea of commodity fetishism. For Marx the market is not as fair as we usually think; we are entering the market-place from different situations, with differing assets, interests, wants and needs, and this distorts the relation between the use-value and the exchange-value. In a similar vein, we all come from different situations as legal subjects, and this distorts the "objectivity" of formal equality. At the moment of exchange there is a need for equal recognition, free will, and rightful ownership, but very few transactions are fully just and fulfill these parameters. Forced coercion, desperate need, exploitation or marginalization disrupts the fairness of a transaction. Similarly it distorts formal rights:

> Just as the commodity was transformed from use-value to exchange value, so too is the person. Differences have been brought under the relationship of equivalence. Pushed away from consciousness is not only the unique and idiosyncratic, but also the historical production of the commodity and the person. (Pashukanis 2003: xiii)

To Pashukanis, our rights are just like our possessions are commodities. We come to consume law and our societal position. These situations emerge from an unfair distribution of goods and rights, although this fact is pushed away from our consciousness. Power manages to "extract and enforce" eternal conditions of ownership and legal rights beyond our particular historical conditions: "Legal fetishism complements commodity fetishism." (Pashukanis 2003: 117)

Activist and scholar Grace Lee Boggs has discussed similar issues at length. The democratization of consumer culture has paradoxically also made us treat democracy as a commodity. We vote with our dollars, but also pay with our votes. We have forgotten how to practice true democracy:

> The problem is that our debate is confined to narrow parameters. Too often we regard health care and education as commodities, and we remain complicit as our elected representatives reduce us to consumers. We forgo an opportunity to debate and discuss real solutions to the crises at hand. Instead of focusing directly on the issue of health care, our political discourse centers on health insurance programs that have more to do with feeding the already monstrous medical-industrial complex than with our physical, mental and spiritual health. (Boggs 2012: 77)

A similar conclusion is advanced by social justice writer Raj Patel in his book *The Value of Nothing* (2009). Here he observes that "under capitalism, *money is the right to have rights*" and continues, "the gap between what people earn and the cost of their freedoms means that, for more and more Americans, freedom is just another word for nothing they can afford." (Patel 2009: 113) Through consumer society we thus feel free, but we are never exposed to the paradox of how it costs us more and more to be as "free" as we were at the start, as the strife for positional goods keeps growing. Patel puts it elegantly: "Economy is about choices. But it is never said who gets to make them." (Patel 2009: 146)

We thus need to widen our everyday understanding of the concept of "democratization" and move it beyond consumerism to include perspectives of social justice. Highlighted by political researcher John Alexander, democracy is much more than free and fair elections. It also requires a functioning democratic government, vibrant opposition parties, a free and critical press, freedom of speech and assembly – which all contribute to many socially desirable goals. But most importantly, "democratic rights do not have derivative importance in terms of what they contribute to social goals, but rather they have their intrinsic importance." (Alexander 2008: 13) Democracy from this perspective is thus not a question of utility maximization, but of autonomy, well-being and the right to self-determination and self-definition. This is thus a perspective on democracy much larger than the limited choice offered through the commodity economy. To better expose how we can address social justice in fashion the Greek philosopher Cornelius Castoriadis' concepts of autonomy and heteronomy can be put in relation to fashion and its laws or "logic" – the *nomos* for fashion.

For Castoriadis autonomous societies are those in which their members are explicitly *self-instituting* their own laws. In contrast, the members of heteronomous societies attribute their imaginaries to some extra-social authority, such as God, tradition, ancestors, or perhaps even divine designers. From Castoriadis' perspective, fashion could be seen as a regime of *instituted heteronomy*. Fashion is a kind of law that is transcendent to society itself, and it is instituted beyond the reach of the citizens. Its basis might lay in the basic human trait of imitation, but it is socially amplified through the nomos and the myth of the creative genius or the star, which produces a *closure of signification*, as if it was a "word of God", beyond discussion or questioning. Ultimately, the role of culture in a democratic society is exactly this; to create the social condition by which we can question the closures of signification and imagination in order to critically reexamine the nomos (Castoriadis 1994).

To Castoriadis, autonomy is the act of explicit self-institution, which Castoriadis traces back to the emergence of the democratic Greek cities and their intimate connection with the early philosophers, specifically the "citizen-philosopher" Socrates rather than elitist-driven Plato (Castoriadis 1991: 6ff). As Castoriadis highlights, it is the explicit self-reflection that lies is the foundation of democracy,

> The struggle for democracy is the struggle for true self-government. As the aim of self-government is not to accept external limits, true self-government entails explicit self-institution, which presupposes, of course, the putting into question of the existing institution—and this, in principle, at any time. [...] In other words, democracy is the regime of (political) self-reflectiveness. (Castoriadis 1991: 20f)

But political self-reflection is inter-subjective and collective, and it is a civic act. Castoriadis continues:

> Democracy is the project of breaking the closure at the collective level. Philoso-

> phy, creating self-reflective subjectivity, is the project of breaking the closure at a level of thought [...] Thus, the birth of philosophy is not just coincident, but equisignificant with the birth of democracy. Both are expressions and central embodiments, of the project of autonomy. (Castoriadis 1991: 21)

Democracy from Castoriadis' perspective, has thus nothing to do with "voting with our dollars" through cheap superabundance, or "made for all" by means of cheap mass-production. Instead, it is the conscious act of self-determination and self-reflection, where we ask ourselves, on a collective level, "are our laws just?" and "are these the laws we want?" To Castoriadis, democracy is the "questioning of the law in and through that actual activity of the community. [...] At that moment *politics* is born; that is to say, freedom is born as socio-historically *effective* freedom." (Castoriadis 1991: 164)

Yet, if we are to examine the effective freedom in fashion we may have to look beyond the commodity to instead examine self-reliant fashion from an angle which includes the (external and internal) capabilities for autonomy. For such approach, the "capabilities approach" of Amartya Sen can be of help.

One of Sen's fundamental critiques to our everyday perspective on societal development is that we are too focused on economic growth and the measuring of this development through our access to commodities (Sen 1985). This is also common in fashion, as we usually conceive that owning the fashionable garment immediately transfers its characteristics onto us, making us fashionable. But as Sen argues, possessing a commodity does not mean one knows how to use it:

> Commodities are seen in terms of their characteristics. The characteristics are various desirable properties of the commodities in question. Securing amounts of these commodities gives the person command over the corresponding characteristics. [...] However, the characteristics of the goods do not tell us what the person will be able to do with those properties. [...] In judging the well-being of the person, it would be premature to limit the analysis to the characteristics of goods possessed. (Sen 1985: 9)

Sen argues that we need to shift focus from the commodities, or the inherent characteristics of these objects, to instead look at "what the person succeeds in doing with the commodities and characteristics at his or her command" (Sen 1985: 10).

To Sen, capabilities should be understood as *what a person is able to do and be*. Sen further differentiates between internal and external capabilities, that is, our inner abilities and our opportunities to enact them in the world. As Sen's collaborator, philosopher Martha Nussbaum puts it, capabilities "are not just abilities residing inside a person but also freedoms and opportunities created by a combination of personal abilities and the political, social, and economic environment" (Nussbaum 2011: 20). Yet, as argued by Castoriadis, to have the capabilities to be an autonomous individual is both an issue of civic interdependence as well as a mobilization of the self-reflective tools to institute new perspectives on our social world. This means to recognize the people who are excluded and unaccounted for, the marginalized and disadvantaged, in order to also address their abilities and possible choices.

We thus need to move beyond the limited notion of democracy, simply choosing from pre-determined options, to instead look for a larger participatory and self-reflective mode of interaction with fashion. Perhaps we could strive for what Lappé calls a "living democracy". Instead of a consumer democracy, where we act out of self-defense and fear of losing our position, she proposes proactive micro self-governance. In such self-governance we communally engage to create a social life lived without domination in any form. In Lappé's vision, creative communities form *relational power* by building relationships of trust, analyzing power and self-interest, mobilizing knowledge and taking public action with discipline, persistence and humor (Lappé 2010: 122ff). She identifies the basics for shaping a population's engagement in the "arts of democracy": active listening, creative conflict, mediation, negotiation, political imagination, public dialogue, public judgment, celebration, evaluation and reflection and mentoring (Lappé 2010: 131ff). These are civic qualities we will need to foster within fashion too.

Democracy in fashion means to continuously discuss and reflect on who is counted, who is included and excluded, what "wrongs" have been committed, and what are the just values and laws we want to cultivate. It is an act of self-reflection and self-determination, but it is mostly an act of listening to those who are disadvantaged. If fashion is to take on the attribute of "democratic" it needs more than cheap mass-production. It needs to listen more, proclaim less, become more humble and more helpful. It needs to engage in the relational "arts of democracy" and offer liberation to those in need.

In the end, fashion is a phenomenon happening between us, it is also a *relational power*, but it could be used for our civic goods. It can be a form of beauty distributed throughout the social. As Elaine Scarry has prompted, drawing from Rawls' idea of justice as "a symmetry of everyone's relations to each other" (Scarry 1999: 63) - the symmetry and equality of its proportions are part of the beauty itself. And she notes "that beautiful things give rise to the notion of distribution, to a lifesaving reciprocity, to fairness not just in the sense of loveliness of aspect but in the sense of 'a symmetry of everyone's relations to each other.'" (Scarry 1999: 65)

REFER

# ENCES

Alexander, John (2008) *Capabilities and Social Justice: The Political Philosophy or Amartya Sen and Martha Nussbaum*, Aldershot: Ashgate

Anderson, Benedict (1983) *Imagined communities: reflections on the origin and spread of nationalism*, London: Verso

Ag Apparel, About us, http://www.agapparel.com/index.php?main_page=page&id=5 [accessed Nov 12, 2012]

Arendt, Hannah (1969) *On Violence*, New York: Harcourt

Articulo 6 (2012) www.articulo6.pe [accessed November, 2012]

Asch, Adrienne (1986) "Will populism empower the disabled?" *Social Policy.* 16(3), 12-18.

Bagli, Charles V (2009) "New York Seeks to Consolidate Its Garment District." *The New York Times.* August 19, 2009. http://www.nytimes.com/2009/08/20/nyregion/20garment.html?pagewanted=all&_r=0

Baker, Bob (1988) "Deeply Rooted in L.A. : Chicano Gangs: A History of Violence." *Los Angeles Times* http://articles.latimes.com/1988-12-11/news/mn-429_1_chicano-gang-members/6

Bamber, Scott (2012) *The Women and Wealth Project: Empowering Positive Women through Social Enterprises – Results Assessment.* Bangkok, Thailand: UNDP.

Baudrillard, Jean (1981) *For a critique of the political economy of the sign*, St. Louis: Telos Press

Benjamin, Medea & Jodie Evans (eds) (2005) *Stop the Next War Now: Effective Responses to Violence and Terrorism.* San Francisco: Inner Ocean Publishing, 2005.

Blackman, Inge and Katheryn Perry (1990), "Skirting The Issue: Lesbian Fashion for the 1990s" in Feminist Review, *Perverse Politics: Lesbian Issues*, No. 34, Spring 1990

Blanks, Tim (2011) "Christina Dior Fall 2011 RTW." *Style.com.* 2011. http://www.style.com/fashionshows/review/F2011RTW-CDIOR [accessed Sept 27th, 2012]

Boggs, Grace Lee (2012) *The next American revolution: sustainable activism for the twenty-first century*, Berkeley: University of California Press

Bond, Paul (2012). "2012 Republican Convention: Protesters Dressed as Vaginas Greet Delegates." *The Hollywood Reporter*, August 27, 2012. http://www.hollywoodreporter.com/news/tampa-republican-conventions-code-pink-vagina-protesters-365541 [accessed Oct 29, 2012]

de Botton, Alain (2004) *Status anxiety*, London: Hamish Hamilton

Bourdieu, Pierre (1984) *Distinction: a social critique of the judgement of taste*, London: Routledge

Bufacchi, Vittorio (2007) *Violence and Social Justice*, New York: Palgrave

Cahill, Spencer and Robin Eggleston (1995) "Reconsidering the Stigma of Physical Disability: Wheelchair Use and Public Kindness," *The Sociology Quarterly*, 36:4

Calefato, Patrizia (2004) *The Clothed Body.* New York: Berg

California Green Solutions (2012) "Homeboy Industries - We can learn to love and respect each other." http://www.californiagreensolutions.com/cgi-bin/gt/tpl.h,content=196. [accessed Sept 29, 2012]

Capeheart, Loretta, & Dragan Milovanovic (2007) *Social Justice: Theories, Issues, and Movements*, New Brunswick, NJ: Rutgers University Press

Castoriadis, Cornelius (1992) "Power, Politics and Autonomy" in *Philosophy, Politics and Autonomy*, New York: Oxford University Press

CFDA (2012) "CFDA Health Initiative." http://cfda.com/programs/cfda-health-initiative

Clark, Hazel & Brody, David (2009) *Design Studies: a Reader*, Oxford and New York: Berg

Clean Clothes Campaign (n.d.), "What We Believe ." http://www.cleanclothes.org/about-us/what-we-believe-in. [accessed Oct 1, 2012]

Clements, Erin. "Beyoncé Is the Face of Fashion for Haiti" *Elle.* February 2010. http://www.elle.com/news/culture/beyonce-is-the-face-of-fashion-for-haiti-1211.

CNN (2011) "Shoe company hopes to kick-start manufacturing in Africa." [modified February 1, 2011] http://edition.cnn.com/2011/BUSINESS/02/01/oliberte.shoes.africa/index.html.

Critchell, Samantha (2012) "Vogue Bans Models Who are too Skinny, Underage." *MSNBC News.* May 3, 2012. http://today.msnbc.msn.com/id/47286154/ns/today-%20style/t/vogue-bans-models-who-are-too-skinny-underage/#.UImv2LT2kyF

Davies, Lizzy (2009) "Seamstress Takes on Might of Chanel over Crochet Pattern." *The-Guardian.co.uk.* 2009. http://www.guardian.co.uk/lifeandstyle/2009/nov/05/seamstress-takes-on-chanel [accessed Sept 26th, 2012]

Doctors Without Borders USA (2012) "About Us" http://www.doctorswithoutborders.org/aboutus [accessed Nov 14, 2012]

Domenighini, Annalise (2012). "Vagina Brigade, Other Join Forces to Begin Protesting theRepublican National Convention." *The Bottom Line* (UCSB), August 27, 2012. http://thebottomline.as.ucsb.edu/2012/08/vagina-brigade-others-join-forces-to-begin-protesting-the-republican-national-convention [accessed Oct 29, 2012]

Downs Designs (n.d.) http://www.downsdesigns.com [accessed Sept 29, 2012]

Dress For Success (n.d.) "What we Do", http://www.dressforsuccess.org/whatwedo.aspx [accessed Nov. 12, 2012]

Dworkin, Ronald (1977) *Taking rights seriously,* London: Duckworth

Ellis, Adrian & Anthony Heath (1983) "Positional Competition, or an offer you can't refuse," in Ellis and Kumar (eds) *Dilemmas of Liberal Democracies,* London: Tavistock Publications

Entwistle, Joanne (2000) *The Fashioned Body: Fashion, Dress, and Modern Social Theory.* Cambridge: Polity Press.

Fashion Designers Without Borders (2012) "About Us." http://fashiondesignerswithoutborders.com/about/about-us/ [accessed Oct 25, 2012]

Featherstone, Liza (2004). "Pink Thongs and Patriarchy: In Protests against the Iraq War, Women are Using the Media and Popular Culture as Never Before." *The Women's Review of Books.* 21. no. 12: 11-12.

Feagin, Joe & Hernán Vera (2001) *Liberation sociology,* Boulder: Paradigm.

FEED (2012) FEED Projects. Last modified 2012. http://www.feedprojects.com.

"First Look: Katherine Hamnett's Climate Week T-shirt for H&M" *Grazia.* March 13, 2012. http://www.graziadaily.co.uk/fashion/archive/2012/03/13/first-look--celebs-wear-katherine-hamnetts-climate-week-t-shirt-for-h-m.htm.

Gangs Or Us (2012) "Gang History." [accessed November 10, 2012] http://www.gangsorus.com/gang_history.html.

Fenn, Donna (2010) "Lauren Bush and Ellen Gustafson, Founders of FEED Projects." *Inc.,* July 19, 2010. http://www.inc.com/30under30/2010/profile-lauren-bush-ellen-gustafson-feed-projects.html.

First Friday Book Synopsis (2010) "Interview: Nancy Lubin" http://ffbsccn.wordpress.com/2010/07/23/interview-nancy-lublin/ [accessed Nov 10, 2012]

Garner John V. (2011) "Cornelius Castoriadis." Last modified 2012. http://www.iep.utm.edu/castoria/#SH4a [accessed 19 Nov. 2012]

Garton, Christie (2011) "Feed Projects Line of Bags Help Feed Hungry Kids." *USA Today,* July 17, 2011. http://yourlife.usatoday.com/mind-soul/doing-good/story/2011/07/Feed-Projects-line-of-bags-helps-feed-hungry-kids/49468942/1. [accessed 19 Nov. 2012]

Gilligan, Carol (1982) *In A Different Voice,* London: Harvard University Press

Giroux, Henry (2012) "Hoodie Politics: Trayvon Martin and Racist Violence in Post Racial America." *Truth-out.org* [modified April 2, 2012] http://truth out.org/news/item/8203-hoodie-politics-and-the-death-of-trayvon-martin.

Good.is (2012) "How Oliberté, the Anti-TOMS, Makes Shoes and Jobs in Africa." [modified January 17, 2012] http://www.good.is/posts/how-oliberte-the-anti-toms-makes-shoes-and-jobs-in-africa/

Goods of Conscience (2012) http://www.goodsofconscience.com [accessed 1 Nov, 2012]

Graham, Janna (2007), 'Discussion', in N Monem (ed.) *Lucy + Jorg Orta Pattern Book: An Introduction to Collaborative Practices,* London: Black Dog Publishing

Granata, Francesca (2009) "Multiple Systems and Composite Identities in New York Fashion: An Interview with Mary Ping." *Fashion Practice,* Vol.1, Iss.2

Grazia (2012) "First Look: Katherine Hamnett's Climate Week T-shirt for H&M" *Grazia.* March 13,2012. http://www.graziadaily.co.uk/fashion/archive/2012/03/13/first-look--celebs-wear-katherine-hamnetts-climate-week-t-shirt-for-h-m.htm

Greenhouse, Steven (1989), "Paris Talks Seek Attention for Plight of Kurds" *The New York Times,* 15 Oct, http://www.nytimes.com/1989/10/15/world/paris-talks-seekattention-for-plight-of-kurds.html?ref=kurds [accessed 10 Nov, 2012]

Guzman Bouvard, Marguerite (1994). *Revolutionizing Motherhood: The Mothers of the Plaza de Mayo. Wilmington,* DE: Scholarly Resources.

Ha, Julie and David Kim. "Clean Clothes, Big Hearts." *KoreAm.* December 2, 2011. http://iamkoream.com/december-issue-clean-clothes-big-hearts/

Hirsch, Fred (1977) *The Social Limits to Growth,* London: Routledge

Hollander, Anne (1993) *Seeing through clothes,* Berkeley: University of California Press

Hollender, Jeffrey (2012) "Made in Africa." http://www.jeffreyhollender.com/?p=2391. [accessed Oct 24, 2012]

Homeboy Industries (2012) "Homeboy Silkscreen & Embroidery." http://www.homeboyindustries.org/what-we-do/homeboy-silkscreen-embroidery [accessed Sept 29, 2012]

Ides, Matthew A. (2009) "Cruising For Community: Youth Culture and Politics in Los Angeles, 1910-1970." PhD diss., University of Michigan [accessed September 29, 2012].

Inhabitat (2009) "The Green Shows at New York Fashion Week," YouTube video, posted by "Inhabitat," Sept 22, 2009. http://www.youtube.com/watch?v=2M3fVYBsZrw&feature=related

IOU (n.d.) The IOU Project – Introduction http://www.youtube.com/watch?feature=player_embedded&v=Yybe3hB3Ix4, [accessed Oct 26, 2012]

IZ Adaptive, About, http://www.izadaptive.com/about2.aspx [accessed Nov 12, 2012]

Kasmeneo (2012) Flickr Page, http://www.flickr.com/photos/kasmeneo/7692856622/in/photostream [accessed Oct 15, 2012]

Katharine Hamnett (n.d.) http://www.katharinehamnett.com

Kreisinger, Elisa (2012) "Friday Fashion For Feminists: A Queer Act" at *Popculturepirate.com,* http://popculturepirate.com/2012/04/06/friday-fashion-for-feminists-a-queer-act/ [accessed October 15, 2012]

Kutz-Flamenbaum, Rachel (2007). "Code Pink Raging Grannies, and the Missile Dick Chicks: Feminist Performance Activism in the Contemporary Anti-War Movement." *NWSA Journal.* 19. no. 1: 89-105.

Lagerfeld, Karl (2007) *Lagerfeld Confidential,* movie by Rodolphe Marconi

Lappé, Frances Moore (2010) *Getting a grip 2: clarity, creativity and courage for the world we really want,* Cambridge: Small Planet Media

Larrabee, Mary Jeanne (1993) *An Ethic of Care,* New York and London: Routledge

LeBesco, Kathleen (2004) *Revolting Bodies? The Struggle to Redefine Fat Identity.* Amherst and Boston: University of Massachusetts Press

Lee, Han (2012) Oral Interview with Minna Shim. New York, NY., September 26th, 2012.

Lee, Michele (2003) *Fashion Victim: Our Love-Hate Relationship with Dressing, Shopping, and the Cost of Style,* New York: Broadway Books

Lerner, Michael (1986) *Surplus powerlessness: the psychodynamics of everyday life and the psychology of individual and social transformation,* Oakland, CA: Institute for Labor and Mental Health

Linard, Emmanuelle (2012) "Fashion designers without borders." Trend Tablet http://www.trendtablet.com/11773-fashion-designers-without-borders/#.T-lQ9jT8acY.facebook [accessed Oct 25, 2012]

Local Wisdom (2012) http://www.localwisdom.info

Made in Midtown (2010) http://www.madeinmidtown.org/#made-in-midtown

Marimacho (n.d.) Marimachobk.com, http://marimachobk.com/about/ [accessed October 15, 2012]

Mccue, Matt , "Man of the Cloth, and the Runway" The Wall Street Journal, 15 October, http://blogs.wsj.com/metropolis/2012/02/09/a-man-of-the-cloth-works-therunway/ [accessed 10 Nov, 2012]

Melago, Carrie (2009) "Ralph Lauren Model Filippa Hamilton: I was fired because I was too fat!" *New York Daily News,* October 18, 2009. http://www.nydailynews.com/life-style/fashion/ralph-lauren-model-filippa-hamilton-i-fired-i-fat-article-1.381093 [accessed Sept 27, 2012]

Molloy, Joanna (2009) "Bronx Priest Rev. Andrew O'Connor Gives Fashion Design and Organic Twist" *New York Daily News,* 5 December, http://articles.nydailynews.com/2009-12-06/local/17940822_1_clothing-line-men-s-suits-vogue [accessed 10 Nov, 2012]

Moon, Christina Harriet (2011) "Material Intimacies: The Labor of Creativity in the Global Fashion Industry." Yale University. Chapter 4.

Mullins, Aimee (2009), "It's not fair having 12 pairs of legs" Speech at TED Conference

National Down Syndrome Society / NDSS (2012) "Down Syndrome Facts." http://www.ndss.org/Down-Syndrome/Down-Syndrome-Facts/

Navarro, Marysa (2001). The Personal is Political: Las Madres de Plaza de Mayo. Power and Popular Protest: Latin American Social Movements. Edited by Susan Eckstein. Los Angeles: University of California Press.

Nedan Foundation (n.d.) http://nedan.in/about [accessed Nov 5, 2012]

New York Daily News (2012) "Plus-size models may boost body image, study says." *New York Daily News,* November 9, 2012. http://www.nydailynews.com/life-style/health/plus-size-models-boost-body-image-study-article-1.1199412 [accessed Nov 16, 2012]

Nussbaum, Martha (2006) *Frontiers of Justice: Disability, Nationality, Species Membership,* Cambridge: Harvard University Press

Nussbaum, Martha (2011) *Creating capabilities: the human development approach,* Cambridge: Belknap

Oliberté (2012) "Story: Behind the Scenes."http://www.oliberte.com/story/ [accessed Oct 24, 2012]

-- "Environment." [accessed Oct 24, 2012] http://www.oliberte.com/story/environment/

-- "Play Fair." [accessed Oct 24, 2012] http://www.oliberte.com/story/play-fair/

-- "Why Africa." [accessed Oct 24, 2012] http://www.oliberte.com/story/why-africa/.

Olins, Alice (2008) "My Life in Fashion: Katharine Hamnett." *The Times.* April 9, 2008.

http://www.thetimes.co.uk/tto/life/fashion/article1752404.ece.

Pagani, Susan (2005). "You've been pink'd: CODEPINK uses humor and politics to make a point." *San Antonio Current,* June 16, 2005.

Pashukanis, Evgeny (2003) *The general theory of law and Marxism,* New Brunswick: Transaction Publishers

Passariello, Christina. "Paris Court Throws Out Forgery Claim Against Chanel." *TheWallStreetJournal.com.* 2009. http://online.wsj.com/article/SB10001424052748704201404574590270596276350.html [accessed Sept 26, 2012]

Ping, Mary (2008) "Mary Ping." Last modified 2008. http://www.maryping.com/

Plato (1989) "Republic" from *The Collected Dialogues of Plato,* ed. Edith Hamilton, Princeton, NJ: Princeton University Press

Pullin, Graham (2009) *Design meets Disability,* Cambridge: MIT Press

Ralph Lauren Media LLC (2012) "About Ralph Lauren" http://global.ralphlauren.com/en-us/about/Pages/default.aspx. [accessed Sept 28, 2012]

Ranciére, Jacques (2004) *The politics of aesthetics,* London: Continuum

Rantisi, Norma (2006) "How New York Stole Modern Fashion." in Breward & Gilbert (eds) *Fashion's World Cities,* Oxford & New York: Berg Publishers.

Raphael, Rina (2012) "Eco-Friendly Designer Diaper Bags: Lauren Bush Lauren's Chic Activism." *MSNBC.com,* September 7, 2012. http://today.msnbc.msn.com/id/48930484/ns/today-style/t/eco-friendly-designer-diaper-bags-lauren-bush-laurens-chic-activism/#.UJVBwLTxAyE

Rawls, John (1999) *A theory of justice,* Oxford: Oxford University Press

Roberts, Sam (2011) "One in Five New York City Residents Living in Poverty" *The New York Times,* 22 September, [accessed 10 Nov, 2012] http://www.nytimes.com/2011/09/22/nyregion/one-infive-new-york-city-residents-living-in-poverty.html?_r=0

Sandel, Michael (2009) *Justice: What's the Right Thing to Do?* New York: Farrar, Strauss and Giroux

Save the Garment Center (SGC) (2012) Last modified 2012. http://savethegarmentcenter.org.

Scarry, Elaine (1999) *On beauty and being just,* Princeton: Princeton University Press

Sen, Amartya (1992) *Inequality reexamined,* Oxford: Oxford University Press

Sen, Amartya (2008) "The Idea of Justice." *Journal of Human Development* 9, no. 3 (November 2008): 331-342.

Siek, Stephanie (2011) "A Perfect Fit for Those With Down Syndrome." *CNN.* December 11,2011. http://inamerica.blogs.cnn.com/2011/12/11/a-perfect-fit-for-those-with-down-syndrome/

Sjoberg, Gideon, Elizabeth Gill & Leonard Cain (2003) "Countersystem Analysis and the Construction of Alternative Futures", *Sociological Theory,* Volume 21, Issue 3

Slow and Steady Wins the Race (2012) "Slow and Steady Wins the Race." http://www.slowandsteadywinstherace.com/pages/about-us

Smith, Marquard & Morra, Joanne (2006) *The Prosthetic Impulse: From a Posthuman Present to a Biocultural Future,* Cambridge: MIT Press

Thesocietypages.org (2009) http://thesocietypages.org/socimages/2009/05/03/rejecting-the-gender-binary-in-fashion/ [accessed Oct 15, 2012]

Stand Up To Cancer (2012) "What is S2UC?" http://www.standup2cancer.org/what_is_su2c

Styles, Ruth. "The Ecologist Meets...Katharine Hamnett." *The Ecologist.* March 13, 2012. http://www.theecologist.org/green_green_living/clothing/1273787/the_ecologist_meetskatherine_hamnett.html

Sobchack, Vivian (2006) "A Leg to Stand on: Prosthetics, Metaphor, and Materiality", in Smith, Marquard and Morra, Joanne, *The Prosthetic Impulse: From a Posthuman Present to a Biocultural Future,* Cambridge: the MIT Press, pp. 17-41.

The Supply Change (2012) http://thesupplychange.org [accessed Oct 24, 2012]

Targeted News (2010). "Women Weavers in India Walk out of Vulnerability with Fashion Designer." *Targeted News Service* (Washington, D.C.), June 8, 2010. https://login.libproxy.newschool.edu/login?url=http://search.proquest.com/docview/365827596?accountid=12261 [accessed Nov 5, 2012].

Taylor, Diana (2001) "Making a Spectacle: The Mothers of the Plaza de Mayo." *Journal of the Association for Research on Mothering.* 3. no. 2: 97-109.

The Telegraph (2010) "Bibi Hunts for Natural Weaves in Bodo Heartland- Use of Vivid Colours and Exotic Patterns Bowls over Bangladesh-Born Designer and UN Envoy." *The Telegraph* (Calcutta, India), June 3, 2010. http://www.telegraphindia.com/1100603/jsp/northeast/story_12515382.jsp [accessed Nov 5, 2012]

The Tiffany & Co. Foundation (2012) "The Tiffany & Co. Foundation." http://www.tiffanyandcofoundation.org/

Tiffany & Co. (2012) "Tiffany & Co. Corporate Responsibility." http://www.tiffany.com/CSR .

Tai, Earl (2009) "A Case for Distributive Justice in Design" in Brody & Clark (eds) *Design Studies, a Reader,* Oxford: Berg, Pp. 454-458.

Turner-Bowker, Diane M. (2001) "How Can You Pull Yourself Up by Your Bootstraps, if you Don't have Boots? Work-Appropriate Clothing for Poor Women."*Journal of Social Sciences.* 57:2,

United Nations Development Programme (2012) "HIV-Positive Women Weavers Team up withFashion Designer."

http://www.undp.org/content/undp/en/home/ourwork/hiv-aids/successstories/HIV-women-team-fashion-designer/ [accessed Nov 5, 2012]

United States Census Bureau (2012) U.S. Department of Commerce, [accessed 1 Nov 2012] http://quickfacts.census.gov/qfd/states/36/36005.html

Wanders, Anne Theresia (2010) *Slow Fashion,* Sulgen: Niggli

West, Guida & Rhodia Lois Blumberg (eds) (1990) *Women and Social Protest,* New York: Oxford University Press.

Wilkinson, Isabel (2012) "Ralph Lauren Hires First Plus-Size Model Robyn Lawley." *The Daily Beast,* September 19, 2012. http://www.thedailybeast.com/articles/2012/09/19/ralph-lauren-hires-first-plus-size-model-robyn-lawley.html. [accessed Sept 24, 2012]

Wilson, Elizabeth (2007) *Adorned in Dreams.* London: I.B. Tauris

Wilson, Eric (2012) "Checking Models' IDs at the Door." *The New York Times.* February 8, 2012. http://www.nytimes.com/2012/02/09/fashion/efforts-to-stop-use-of-underage-models-during-new-york-fashion-week.html?pagewanted=all&_r=0.

Wintour, Anna (2012) "Taking a Stand: International Vogue Editors Join Forces to Support the CFDA's Health Initiative." *Vogue.* June 2012.

Wodiczko, Krzysztof (1999) *Critical Vehicles: Writings, Projects, Interviews,* Cambridge: MIT Press.

Wolin, Sheldon (2008) *Democracy incorporated: Managed democracy and the specter of inverted totalitarianism,* Princeton: Princeton University Press

Ziff, Sara. (2012) "Testimony to the New York State Department of Labor." *The Model Alliance.* September 20, 2012. http://modelalliance.org/2012/testimony-to-the-new-york-state-department-of-labor/testimony-to-the-new-york-state-department-of-labor.

Zizek, Slavoj (2009) "First as Tragedy, Then as Farce." Presentation at the Royal Society for the encouragement of Arts, Manufactures and Commerce, London, UK, November 24, 2009.

24844232R00123

Printed in Great Britain
by Amazon